Choices and Challenges:
Charting Your Career Path

Fourth Edition

CHIEF EDITORS

Olivia Martinez   Lorenda Schrader

ASSISTANT EDITORS

Daniel Pascoe   Karen Weist   Jan Van Dyke

DESIGN AND FORMAT

Karla Dunn

Choices and Challenges:

Charting Your Career Path

Dedicated to Alan McNabb, Director of the Career Development Center at Indiana University for 20 years. Alan, thank you for your many contributions to IU and the vision you had for this book and our center.

Acknowledgements

After a long and arduous year of planning, reviewing, editing, consulting and writing, I am pleased to present this career planning textbook to the students at Indiana University and to all students who are in the process of exploring majors and careers.

The completion of this book required the time and efforts of many talented professionals and the patience of many outside consultants. Current and former Indiana University Career Development Center staff members contributed to the success of this edition.

I would like to thank the following individuals who took the time to review this book in the various stages until its completion. Thank you for your time and efforts on the textbook review committee. Our book is improved because of your input, ideas and suggestions and I could not have accepted this project without your help:

Lorenda Schrader, Karen Weist, Daniel Pascoe, Loretta Saunders, Jan Van Dyke, and John Hughey.

I would also like to thank others who were consulted and contributed their time along the different stages of the book:

Laura Dominguez-Chan at Stanford University's Career Development Center and Hortencia Gonzalez of Consulting Psychologist Press. Thank you both for your patience and consultation.

Karen Wright (Indiana University), thank you for the time you spent advising me throughout the process.

Arlene Hill and Sloane Boyd (Indiana University), thank you for comments on several chapters.

Lou Ann Hanson (Indiana University), thank you for the administrative work you did to help speed the progress of this book.

I want to express my deepest gratitude to my husband, Manuel Martinez. Thank you for the sounding board, your patience throughout this process and for volunteering your time and comments.

I would be remiss if I did not mention all of the staff members of the Career Development Center (past and present) who worked on the 1st, 2nd, and 3rd editions of this book. The work they started was instrumental to the content and format of this new edition. Thank you for your creative ideas and traditions you have passed along in this book:

David Ortiz	Heather Wallace
Sue Sgambelluri	Sally Gerrish
Christine Olinger	Janice Wiggins
Kristen Lettington	Paul Timmins
Julia Reed	Jan Nickless

The following individuals must be mentioned because they have contributed to the ideas in this book, specifically the additional resources section. Thank you for your collaboration and ideas and your commitment to assisting students with their career planning these past few years:

Jennifer DeSana	Jennifer Berson
Brad Mulley	Joe Testani
Amy Hollimon	Jeremy Podany
Richard Browne	Joanna Adler
Karen Weist	Daniel Pascoe

The final stages of this book involved extensive work with Karla Dunn, who finalized the visual format of this book and Cathy Parker from Indiana University's Custom Publishing.

Last but not least, I would like thank my director, Dr. Alan McNabb for entrusting me with this challenging and worthwhile project. I am grateful for your encouragement and guidance these past three years. Your contributions to our views and philosophies on career development have shaped the ways in which we assist students at Indiana University.

Olivia Martinez
Associate Director
Career Development Center

Table of Contents

Choices and Challenges:
Charting Your Career Path

Effective Career Planning

What It Can Mean to Your Success

By Olivia Martinez

IN THIS CHAPTER YOU WILL:

➤ Be introduced to the Career Development Stages

➤ Create a vocational autobiography through a personal career essay

➤ Begin the Career Exploration Process

Effective Career Planning

> "Choose a job you love, and you will never have to work a day in your life."
>
> —*Confucius*

What It Can Mean to Your Success

Confucius' statement is easier said than done. Some people report feeling unfulfilled at work, or are dissatisfied with their career choices, so much so that they dream of retirement as the time in their lives when they will be able to do what they *really* want. Would you like to be happy at work? You have seen your parents, grandparents, or guardians come home from their respective jobs and express their feelings about their work. If they have not directly spoken to you about what they do all day you may have assumed a few things: either they are very fulfilled with their work and talk very positively about their experiences or they spend too much time at work or must not enjoy what they do much if they complain and seem dissatisfied. Being happy at one's work requires finding satisfaction with what that vocation entails. According to Super (1996), "Work satisfactions and life satisfactions depend on the extent to which the individual finds adequate outlets for abilities, interests, personality traits, and values."

> "Every man's work . . . is always a portrait of himself."
>
> —*Butler*

This textbook is dedicated to the project of helping you find a vocation that will be an accurate portrait of your deepest interests, a career that challenges you in important ways and acts as a forum for personal expression. There are many difficult questions that you might be facing now: What will I major in? What is my plan now that I'm in college? What will I do with my major? Will I be fulfilled in my career? Will I make enough money? Will I be happy?

As you talk with fellow students, the questions might seem to take on an added urgency. Does everyone in your dorm seem to have a plan for his/her future? Do you feel as if you have to make something up when someone asks you so you don't feel left out? It's not a good feeling to not know what your next step will be. We understand that feeling and would like to help you chart your path toward your future. We also want you to know that these feelings are normal. We hope that through the exercises in this book you will come to realize that you have some time and some important steps to take in order to make an informed decision about your future.

To create good plans, first you must understand why it is important to plan, where to begin and what is involved in the planning. Career development begins and ends with you and it is a life-long, cyclical process. The stages of career development will repeat themselves as you find yourself in the questioning stages of new beginnings from time to time in life.

Career Planning Stages

The following is an outline of the Career Development Stages by Donald Super, one of the foremost career theorists, and some additional information (in italics) to help you implement the stages throughout your college career:

(Super, 1996)

Stage One: Growth

Develop physically and intellectually.

Observe and learn from others around you.

Begin to see yourself as an individual with talents and skills (self-concept).

Stage Two: Exploration

Write down a list of potential careers and majors.

Assess and articulate your personal interests, values, and skills (with advisors, professors and career counselors).

Discover decision-making styles and implement effective decisions (examine your own style and determine the most effective style for career planning).

Take courses that relate to your interests.

Explore careers through part-time work, internships, and research.

Research the required skills and training for your potential career.

Recognize fields most closely related to your interests, values, and skills and add them to your list.

Seek ways to build skills in areas that need to be developed.

Acquire an entry-level position in your chosen field.

Stage Three: Establishment

Create a sense of personal satisfaction in your vocation (include components that satisfy your personal growth—revisit values).

Grow into your position, move up, and accept extra responsibilities.

Stage Four: Maintenance

Continue to grow in your position by accepting additional responsibilities and challenges.

Consider different careers that fit your needs /self-concept.

Stage Five: Disengagement

Retire.

Envision life after work and develop a plan (re-evaluate your needs with a career consultant).

Volunteer in areas that interest you.

Participate in activities that give you energy.

Remember, you may find yourself re-evaluating these stages throughout your life.

Career Planning and Its Importance

Why is career planning important? Think about all the questions you have about your future. Your future encompasses your work, your personal life, your spiritual self, your physical self, and your self-concept. Who are you? Self-concept is an awareness of: how you view yourself, how others view you, what you expect to be (your dreams and ideals), and an awareness of your overall worth.

Effective career planning must and should begin with an awareness of your own self-concept: your interests, abilities, personality, weaknesses, relationships, dreams, goals, influences, etc. Throughout this book, you will have the opportunity to clarify your self-concept through a variety of exercises and to apply this self information to a range of career options that are available to you.

What did you dream of becoming when you were a child? Who or what were your influences? Other people's views of you may have affected your vocational self-concept. Our first vocational impressions often come from people we admire as children like our first-grade teachers, "super heroes," doctors, dads, moms, uncles, aunts, characters in movies, etc. According to Dr. Super, these feelings may have had an influence in our first impressions of careers or dreams we could potentially pursue.

If your parents, teachers, siblings, and friends gave you the idea that things were possible for you, you might have felt empowered to pursue certain things. On the flip side, if these valued people in your life discouraged you or if you tried and failed, you might have been discouraged in your pursuits and began to change your vocational self-concept.

Through your own experiences and as you better understand your own skills, interests and preferences, the first impressions for careers to pursue begin to change. In your mind, you are practicing career development. You are assessing your own abilities, and preferences and then matching them to careers that capture your attention.

Consider James's Story

When James was four years old, he wanted to grow up and become a basketball player. His parents encouraged him throughout his elementary school years by enrolling him in basketball little leagues, attending his basketball games and providing support and verbal encouragement. He was smart and excelled at most subjects throughout school years. Basketball was a major part of his life and James's first choice for a career.

Because of the positive influence of his uncle John, James had also considered becoming a lawyer. James's parents always spoke with such a high

regard for Uncle John. He remembers seeing his uncle from time to time, and he always had exciting stories about his job and seemed very self-confident. When he thought of his uncle John, the words "powerful and influential" came to mind.

At the age of 16, James realized that he was not skilled enough to play in the NBA. He had made it onto the junior varsity team but didn't make it onto the varsity team. His skills were not quite at the level that he needed to be at and his coach had a candid conversation with James about his potential as a professional athlete. It was becoming clear to James that his dream of becoming a professional basketball player was not realistic and that he needed to rethink his career dreams. For James, the process of career development was just beginning. Now he would need to begin exploring other options and begin carefully considering his future. A few trips to the career counselor in his high school would help James begin a new plan of action.

On page 6 is an exercise to help you as you begin to search and understand your own self-concept.

PERSONAL CAREER ESSAY

After learning about the stages of career development, and how you begin to identify with careers as a child and throughout your adolescence, you may want to jot down some notes as to how you have developed your ideas for careers. The following exercise will allow you to track your career path. At what age did you begin to dream about becoming a doctor, baseball player, chemist, veterinarian, lawyer, writer, etc.?

Reflect on past experiences as a child, adolescent, adult, with role models, part-time work, volunteer work, hobbies, high school activities (clubs, athletics, student government), and identify those experiences that have helped you learn about your interests and have given you a picture of what you may want to pursue as a career. The paper should be one to two pages and double-spaced.

Use the following questions to assist you in writing your vocational autobiography:

• What were some of your first visions of careers that you would pursue?

• Have there been any significant experiences in your life that have influenced your chosen career/major interests (ex. parents, teachers, mentors, coaches, etc.)?

• Have your cultural background, socioeconomic status, gender or religious beliefs had any influence in your thoughts about careers or majors?

• Who are your heroes?

• What do you naturally do well?

• What classes fascinate and absorb you?

• What courses have you taken that you did not enjoy?

• When you daydream, what do you see yourself doing?

• What is your definition of success?

• What motivates you?

• What have been your most important learning experiences?

• What is the most gratifying thing that you have ever done? The most dissatisfying?

• What do you think you will need in a job to make you happy?

• What areas about your self would you like to improve?

• What are some of your biggest fears about choosing a major or career?

New Trends Affect Job Choices

Twenty years ago your parents may have studied for one particular profession. They may have started teaching, joined the armed forces or climbed the company ladders through hard work and promotions, and stayed in those professions until retirement. Work trends are changing. According to the Labor Department statistics (*Wall Street Journal*, Careers Section, 1995), the average person will work for more than 10-12 employers, have 3-5 different careers and change jobs at least every 4-5 years. These statistics can be an overwhelming on one hand, but, on the other, it can mean variety, change and challenge throughout your work life.

Because of this new trend, you must begin to think about your plans earlier and more thoroughly. Beginning to think about your career development as early as your freshman or sophomore year in college is worthwhile and smart. So as you begin to plan for your college career you should plan as if you are going on a long and adventurous journey.

Finding Your Way

Think of career planning as a kind of search through a huge array of sometimes confusing choices. Imagine you are at a large, mega-mall. You are in search of a particular store. Perhaps it is a specialty store. As you enter the mall, there are directories in almost every corner or hall entrance. The first thing you do is orient yourself. "You are here," the map asserts helpfully. Next, you want to find the name of the store you are looking to find, and then you want to chart your course from where you are located to where you want to go.

This book will take you through a similar mapping process. As mentioned earlier, career development is a life-long process and it begins with awareness. Understanding who and where you are, your likes and dislikes (interests); determining what skills you have, need and want to develop, what work values you have, and what personality preferences you have, is essential information that you must

---

Career Exploration and Making Informed Decisions Involves:

- Understanding who you are (assessment of your own skills, interests and values)
- Knowing and understanding educational requirements and options
  - requirements for majors, minors and concentrations
  - prerequisites for admissions
  - how majors relate to careers
  - experiential opportunities (internships, volunteer work, etc.)
- Understanding the workplace
  - job responsibilities, tasks and skills
  - salary and job outlook
  - educational requirements for the field
- Researching employers
  - company or organization research
  - knowing what each offers; does it match with your own preferences

---

gather as you make informed decisions regarding your career or major choice.

Information, Decisions and Planning

Information gathering, another important piece of the Career Exploration Process, can entail a lot of work. The more information you gather, the better informed you will be as you begin to narrow down your options. Narrowing your options is essential. This may be difficult for those of you who like to keep all of your options open. If you are one of these people, pay close attention to the guidance in the decision-making chapter and keep in contact with your career counselor at your university or college. You can be skilled at many things, but you will want to find the best fit to include all of your needs (interests, values, skills, personality preferences), so that you are satisfied with your career choices.

The last step of the Career Exploration Process is to develop a plan of action. You will need to be motivated. The key to motivation is to set goals. In Section III of this book, "Taking Action: How can you move forward?," you will learn the importance of making decisions, setting goals, and creating an action plan for your future.

We are pleased to help you on this exciting and adventurous journey and are committed to helping you set up a plan that will lead you to find answers to a dizzying array of questions about your future. After completing this book and making some trips to research and discuss your plans with a career counselor, you will find that you have started on the road to effective career planning. Get ready to learn about yourself and to explore the opportunities that await you!

PART I

Self Assessment: Who Are You?

Career Exploration Process

SELF-INFORMATION

Self-Concept
Values
Skills
Interests
Personality Style
Decision-Making Style

EDUCATIONAL INFORMATION

Majors/Minors
Concentrations
Prerequisites for Admission
Course Requirements
Experiential Education
Campus and Community Resources

WORLD OF WORK INFORMATION

Types of Jobs
Nature of Work
Work Environments
Educational Requirements
Skill Requirements
Employment Outlook

C
A
R
E
E
R

Clarifying and Assessing Your Values

What's Important to You?
By Arlene Hill

IN THIS CHAPTER YOU WILL:

➤ Explore your personal values and their impact on career choice

➤ Understand the meaning of work values and their relationship to careers

➤ Identify and prioritize your top work values

➤ Understand that values change and may even conflict throughout your life

CHAPTER 1
Clarifying and Assessing Your Values

Your values are the sets of beliefs, attitudes, and commitments that underlie your decision-making process; values are the reflection of how you create meaning in life. You are continually in the process of forming and re-evaluating your values based on knowledge and prior experiences, as well as input from parents, friends, organizations, education, etc. Typically, you are happiest when your actions match your values. Unfortunately, because value systems are complex, you frequently need to create a hierarchy of your values to make good decisions.

Sound confusing? You go through this process multiple times every day.

For example, let's say your friends want you to go to a concert tonight, but you have an exam early tomorrow morning and you haven't studied yet. You value their friendship, but you also value achievement and getting good grades. How do you solve this? Most likely, you create a solution that allows you to stay true to your values (stay in studying tonight but go out with those friends tomorrow night). In order to make this decision, you had to weigh the results of each action against your values and decide which value was more important in the short-term (getting good grades or maintaining social connections).

How do you know what you value?

One clue to identifying your values is to assess how you spend your time, energy, and money. The following questions will help you in identifying your values:

1. Of your accomplishments, which one are you most proud? Why?

2. What would you most like to accomplish before you die?

3. If you could change one thing about yourself, what would it be?

4. If you could change one thing in the world, what would it be?

5. To which charities would you most like to donate?

6. If you were not constricted by time or money, what would you most like to learn?

What's Important to You?

> "Far and away the best prize that life offers is the chance to work hard at work worth doing."
>
> —*Theodore Roosevelt*

In choosing a career, it is important to understand your values, and choose work and work environments that best match your values. Examples of work-related values include: helping others, creativity, prestige, security, independence, power, money, variety and many others. The next exercise will assist you in defining, understanding, and assessing your own values in relation to possible careers.

Vocations, Avocations—What's the Difference?

Vocation is the work you do to earn money and provide for yourself. An avocation is work done for the sheer joy of doing it; an avocation is a hobby performed with passion and commitment that is not a primary source of income. Sometimes the solution of balancing passion and lifestyle is to make the passion an avocation, and pursue a career in another field that is interesting and fulfilling, but not a major passion.

Many artists, musicians and athletes find themselves in this situation. *I love to sing; I only feel truly alive when I am singing. But I really need stability. I know I want to have a certain amount of money in my life; I hate feeling like I'm broke. How can I balance my love for singing with a need for stability? HELP!*

There are many ways to find this balance, which is essential for a fulfilling, enjoyable life. Many people pursuing their passion have a "day job," a job that pays the bills and leaves them plenty of time for pursuing their avocation. These "day jobs" take many forms; the best "day job" is one that fits your skills, values, and interests without making too many demands. For Wallace Stevens, 20th century poet, his "day job" was being a vice president at a large insurance firm. When I was acting in Chicago, I chose to work in a corporate job, because I wanted a good salary and benefits; my roommate refused to be tied to an office and worked as a waitress. Both of these "day jobs" were good choices, because they allowed us to have work that fulfilled our needs and enabled us to pursue our acting careers. Of course, the best thing about a "day job" is when you can quit, knowing that your avocation has become a vocation and you can support yourself solely on what you love doing.

Another option is to go directly for your dreams without compromising. Consider Michael: Michael refused to do any kind of work that wasn't related to acting. He did all kinds of things to earn his living: human mannequin work, singing telegrams, and (my favorite) being a talking reindeer head on a banquet table for a holiday party. While it wasn't stable and it was often hard work, he supported himself and was happy with his freedom and independence.

Before deciding to make your passion a vocation, understand your values. If you value security and stability, freelance work will be incredibly stressful, despite how rewarding you find the job. The pressure to find work may keep you from enjoying the work when you get it. If you know that you value your passion above all other values, go for it. Keep in mind that in most situations you will have to compromise, and know what compromises you are willing to make.

Remember, too, that your interests, skills, and values will constantly be changing, and you may have to continually re-evaluate your choices. The good and bad news is that you can change your mind any time and go another direction!

—Arlene Hill

Exercise

VALUES

Rate each of the following values based on how important you would like each to be in your work using the following scale:

1 = Not Important At All   2 = Not Very Important

3 = Somewhat Important   4 = Very Important

Category I: Content of Work

3   My work is **challenging.**

2   My work involves **decision-making.**

4   I have **autonomy** in my work; I set my own work priorities.

4   My work requires me to be a **leader** or supervisor to others.

3   My work is **detail-oriented.**

3   My work is **intellectually stimulating.**

2   My work requires much **creativity.**

4   I am **continually learning** on the job.

4   My work **contributes to others'** well-being and helps others.

1   There are many **deadlines** and **pressures** in my work.

2   My work has much **variety.**

3   My work entails much **self-expression.**

2   My work requires a high level of **responsibility** for others.

1   My work **involves risk.**

2   My work includes **much adventure.**

2   I do the same daily **routine** in my work.

Category II: Benefits of My Work

4   I earn a **large salary** for my work.

4   People **respect** me for the work that I do.

3   There is room for **advancement** and **promotion.**

3   My work has **integrity.**

4   I am perceived as **influential** or **powerful** because of my position.

4   My work **gives back** to the community.

4   People **admire** or look up to **me** for the work I do.

Category III: My Work Environment

4   My workday is **flexible,** and I can set my own schedule.

3   It is quiet so I can **focus on my work.**

4   There is **diversity** among the people with whom I work.

2   I work **indoors** in a pleasant setting.

2   My work environment is **fast-paced.**

4   I am **safe** in my work environment.

3   The pace where I work is **relaxed.**

3   I work with the public frequently; I interact with **many people.**

3   My workday is **predictable.**

2   I work **outdoors.**

Category IV: The People with Whom I Work

2   I **work frequently** with **co-workers** in teams.

4   I **trust** my co-workers.

2   My colleagues and I are very **competitive.**

4   There is **harmony** among my colleagues.

4   My co-workers **care** about me.

4   **Humor** is important to my colleagues and me.

2   My colleagues are very **similar to me.**

3   My co-workers are **loyal.**

2   My colleagues let me work **on my own** and do not interrupt me when I am working.

3   My colleagues appreciate **individualism.**

3   My colleagues differ from me, and I learn from our **differences.**

Exercise

Once you have finished rating each item, review the list to come up with your top 10 values. Consider each value's specific meaning to you.

Value	Specific Meaning to You
Example 1:	
Intellectually Stimulating	I will have to research and learn new ideas as part of my job, as well as present and defend those ideas to co-workers or clients.
Example 2:	
Co-workers in teams	I will get along well with my co-workers, and we will frequently have to work together on projects.

1. Leader _____ _____

2. Contribute's to others _____

3. Large Salary _____

4. Influential / Powerful _____

5. Flexible _____

6. Diversity _____

7. Autonomy _____

8. Continually Learning _____

9. Respect _____

10. Trust _____

– Adapted from Stanford University Career Development Center's "Values Inventory." Anne Greenblatt, 2000

Now, look back at the four categories: Content, Benefits, Environment and People. Which category is most important to you?

In future chapters, as you identify and research careers, keep the most important value category in mind; you will want to make sure that the career path you choose matches well with what you value.

Discovering Your Skills

Assessing Your Strengths and Talents

By Sally Gerrish

IN THIS CHAPTER YOU WILL:

➤ Identify your talents and their relationship to skills

➤ Identify your skills and their relationship to talents

Understand the difference between skills and talents

➤ Understand how identifying your skills and talents will help you in your major and career search

➤ Identify skills you enjoy using and would like to develop

CHAPTER 2
Discovering Your Skills

Talent + Skills + Knowledge = Your Strengths

"Each person's greatest room for growth is in the areas of his or her greatest strengths."

—*Marcus Buckingham and Donald O. Clifton, Ph.D.*

Assessing Your Strengths and Talents

In the process of your career exploration, it is important to identify your interests, clarify your values, assess your skills, and realize your talents. When you recognize your talents, your skills, your education, and your experiences, you can determine your strengths. Taking the time to recognize these areas, and combining this information with your strongest interests, your values, and your personality type, will lead you to explore career areas that will be challenging and satisfying.

Consider that skills are easier to develop if you have the talent to learn them; course work is easier to accomplish if there is interest and a natural ability. How do you begin to learn about your own skills and talents? It is often difficult to distinguish a talent from a skill. *Skills are something you have acquired or learned. They are defined as the ability to do something well, especially as a result of experience.* A talent is a natural ability. *Webster's Dictionary* defines skill as, "A learned power of doing a thing competently." Combining these key elements can lead you to more accurate information about yourself.

To begin recognizing your skills, think about your accomplishments and achievements. What skills have you already developed through course work, part-time jobs, volunteer work, and school activities? For example, you may have been a member of the yearbook staff: what were your tasks on the staff; what is one accomplishment you achieved during your time on the staff? If you have worked a part-time job: what were your tasks; what was a difficult situation you handled; what did you enjoy; what did you dislike? If you have been a member of an organization and were responsible for a large event: what were your tasks; what was an accomplishment; what did you learn? Recognizing skills you have and enjoy using increases your chances of being a more productive and successful person.

> "Once you know your skills, you have the building blocks of your occupation, and with these building blocks, you can define an occupation you love to do."
>
> —*Richard Bolles.*

Exercise

ASSESSING YOUR SKILLS

Think of two activities you are currently doing or have participated in during the past that involve(d) a great deal of energy and focus. Briefly describe the activity, then detail the major tasks, your accomplishments, likes, dislikes, what you learned, etc. Next, write down the skills you developed during this activity. Refer to the skills list on pages 24-25 to help you name your skills. The sample below will also help you brainstorm. As you go through each activity and name your skills, place a check by those skills on p. 24-25 that you have used in your activities. This will help track your skills.

Sample Activity:

As Ropes Director, Kim worked at a girls' camp the summer between her freshmen and sophomore years in college.

Your activities: Use the list on pages 24-25 to identify and name your skills from your activities.

Activity

➤ Ropes Director (Sample)

Tasks

➤ Responsible for the safety of staff and campers in her area

➤ Teach campers and staff safety rules, belaying techniques, and the use of the harness

➤ Motivate campers on ropes course to help challenge them and help them overcome their fears

➤ Create lesson plans for low ropes activities

Activity

➤ _____

Tasks

➤ _____

➤ _____

➤ _____

Activity

➤ _____

Tasks

➤ _____

➤ _____

➤ _____

Exercise

Likes	Dislikes	Skills
➤ Really enjoyed helping campers and staff get past fears and move on to the next step ➤ Really enjoyed being in charge of own area and being in control	➤ Teaching low ropes to younger campers because they don't understand the concept of team building	➤ Leadership ➤ Open to new ideas ➤ Patience!!! ➤ Self-Confidence ➤ Organization

Likes	Dislikes	Skills

➤ _____
   _____
➤ _____
   _____
➤ _____
   _____
	➤ _____
	   _____
	➤ _____
	   _____
	➤ _____
	   _____
		➤ _____
		   _____
		➤ _____
		   _____
		➤ _____
		   _____

Likes	Dislikes	Skills

➤ _____
   _____
➤ _____
   _____
➤ _____
   _____
	➤ _____
	   _____
	➤ _____
	   _____
	➤ _____
	   _____
		➤ _____
		   _____
		➤ _____
		   _____
		➤ _____
		   _____

Evaluate your skills from this exercise. Remember, skills are those things you do well, usually resulting from experience. Most of the skills you have listed are transferable skills. **Transferable skills are those skills that you can use in any career or field regardless of where you have developed them.**

Exercise

YOU HAVE A CHOICE

Let's go a step further and determine what skills you enjoy using the most.

Look through the skills you checked off on pages 24-25. Do some skills come up regularly? Do you find your strongest skills in one or two of the skill categories? Look at each category and determine where most of your skills fall. Do they fall under Management and Administration, Communication, or Research and Investigation? Or do you have a several categories that fit your skills? List the categories that best fit your skills at this time. You can list one or more below:

1._____   2._____

3._____   4._____

Are the skills in the above categories skills you want to build on?

Are there skill categories you would like to develop further?

Place an asterisk (*) next to those skill categories and specific skills you would like to develop further.

As you research careers that you find of interest in your career library on campus or on the web, be sure they include some of your favorite skill categories. For example, counselors work in crisis intervention, rehabilitation, guidance, etc. They are problem-solvers with good communication and counseling skills. Interpersonal skills are a must, and their work can involve working with a range of people from kids to senior citizens, physically challenged or mentally challenged, one on one or on the phone. If you look at the categories on pages 24-25, you will find that counselors match up closely with the communications and human services categories.

You have talent!

Take another look at your list. What do you consider to be your talents, those things that come naturally to you? You say you don't have any? You don't have to be an actor or professional athlete or artist or singer to have natural talents. You have talent. Not sure what your talents are? Here are a few suggestions to start recognizing them:

Ask people who know you. What do they consider your talents to be?

Go back to age 12 or 13. What did you love to do and that made time fly? Did you like to build or create things, play on the computer, sing, dance, play an instrument, play sports, collect things, fix things, tear apart things and put them back together?

The next exercise will allow you to assess your talents.

ASSESSING YOUR TALENTS

Write down three to five natural talents. **These are talents you have *always* had, not skills you have acquired or learned.**

Example:

Talent: I have always had a knack for decorating. My family members and friends always ask my opinion when decorating a room.

Talents:

1. _____

2. _____

3. _____

4. _____

5. _____

How are you using your talents today?

Compare your talents and your skills list. How do your talents complement your skills?

What skills would you like to further develop to enhance your natural talents and abilities?

_____   _____

_____   _____

Adapted from Hire: The Job Hunting/Career-Life Planning Guide, *2nd Edition (Chap. II). Connie Harris, Michael Henle, Michael Stokleton.*

Common Categories of Transferable Skills

Information Management Skills (Arrange and retrieve data, knowledge, ideas)

- Sort data and objects ____
- Compile and rank information ____
- Apply information creatively to specific problems or tasks ____
- Synthesize facts, concepts, and principles ____
- Evaluate information based on appropriate standards ____
- Attend to details ____
- Develop systems ____
- Monitor progress and projects ____
- Streamline systems ____

Design and Planning Skills (Imagine the future and develop a process for creating it)

- Identify alternative courses of action ____
- Set realistic goals ____
- Follow through with a plan or decision ____
- Manage time effectively ____
- Predict future trends and patterns ____
- Accommodate multiple demands for commitment of time, energy and resources ____
- Assess needs ____
- Make and keep a schedule ____
- Set priorities ____

Research and Investigation Skills (The search for knowledge and understanding)

- Use a variety of sources of information ____
- Apply a variety of methods to test the validity of data ____
- Identify problems and needs ____
- Design an experiment, plan, or model that systematically defines a problem ____
- Identify information sources appropriate to special needs or problems ____
- Formulate questions relevant to clarifying a particular problem, topic, or issue ____

Communication Skills (Exchange, transmit, and express knowledge and ideas)

- Listen with objectivity and paraphrase the content of a message ____
- Use various forms and styles of written communication ____
- Speak effectively to individuals and groups ____
- Use various media to present ideas imaginatively ____
- Express one's needs, wants, opinions, and preferences, without offending others ____
- Identify and communicate value judgments effectively ____
- Describe objects or events with few errors ____
- Convey a positive self image to others ____
- Use languages ____
- Work with a variety of groups and people (conversational ability) ____
- Work as part of a team (teamwork) ____

Adapted from Stanford's Printable Worksheets (Functional Skills, Anne Greenblatt) on the Stanford Career Development Web site: http://www.stanford.edu/dept/CDC/graphics/pdfs/TransfSk.pdf

Indiana University Career Development Center

Critical Thinking Skills (Accurately identify the critical issues necessary for making decisions or solving problems)

- Identify a general principle that explains interrelated experiences of factual data   ____
- Define the parameters of a problem   ____
- Identify reasonable criteria for assessing the value of appropriateness of an action or behavior   ____
- Adapt one's concepts and behavior to changing conventions and norms   ____
- Apply appropriate criteria to strategies and action plans   ____
- Take given premises and reason to their conclusion   ____
- Create innovative solutions to complex problems   ____
- Analyze the interrelations of events and ideas from several perspectives   ____

Management and Administration Skills (Direct and guide a group in completing tasks and attaining goals)

- Identify people who can contribute to the solution of a problem or task   ____
- Identify resource materials useful in the solution of a problem   ____
- Delegate responsibility for completion of a task   ____
- Motivate and lead people   ____
- Organize people and tasks to achieve specific goals   ____
- Coordinate people and/or tasks and logistics   ____
- Strategize plans and solutions   ____
- Analyze tasks   ____
- Solve problems   ____
- Make decisions   ____
- Interpret policy   ____
- Give directions   ____
- Resolve conflicts   ____
- Determine and apply policy   ____
- Handle logistics   ____

Human Service Skills (Attend to physical, mental, or social needs of people)

- Employ interpersonal skills   ____
- Attend to people's body language and communications styles   ____
- Ability to empathize   ____
- Demonstrate sensitivity to other's needs   ____
- Counsel individuals on needs and problems   ____
- Advocate for individuals   ____
- Use intuition to assess client needs   ____

Physical Skills (Use hands or tools to build, repair, invent)

- Build, construct, or invent new structures, models, etc.   ____
- Operate equipment   ____
- Use physical coordination   ____
- Restore or repair machinery or structures   ____

Skills Employers Look for in the 21st Century

According to employers responding to Job Outlook 2001, an annual survey conducted by the National Association of Colleges and Employers (NACE), the importance of personal qualities and characteristics in new hires was quite evident. Communication skills—both written and verbal—topped the list; honesty/integrity, teamwork skills, interpersonal skills, and motivation/initiative rounded out the top five. "The "ideal" job candidate knows how to communicate, interact, and work with others effectively." These are the skills liberal arts students build inside and outside the classroom. It is important to take advantage of opportunities to develop these skills and traits. Participate in activities, jobs, and assignments that integrate these skills. It will be time worth spent and an investment that will yield a great return.

The Realization of Your Strengths

How does it feel to know you have skills and talents? You have natural talents that you can utilize during your college years and in your career. You have many skills that you have already learned or acquired from your education and your experiences. You are also beginning to understand what skills you enjoy using. Can these skills enhance your natural talents? Are you proficient in some skills because they are related to your natural talents? What do you feel are areas you would want to develop? These are questions that are central to your

development in college. They will help you to determine what career fields you want to explore.

If you have a natural desire to inquire about theories or facts, or conduct research, you may find that the sciences or social sciences are courses you want to include in your academic planning so that you can develop skills such as analyzing, researching, and problem solving. If you have natural interests and talents in decorating, drawing, and seeing possibilities, you may want to take design classes to further develop your skills. If you have developed skills in working with people and have a desire to help others, you may consider majors in Psychology, Sociology, Anthropology, History, Social Work, English, Communications, Nursing, etc. These are just a few examples.

Combining your skills, values, interests, and personality preferences will be helpful in narrowing your options for careers associated with your majors. Knowing your skills will also help you as you begin your search for employment. Liberal arts students take courses in a wide range of areas. Employers appreciate the diversity of knowledge in different areas. Diversifying your course work can be a way of developing the skills that organizations are seeking.

Understanding Your Interests

What Are Your Passions?

By Allison Keller and Daniel Pascoe

IN THIS CHAPTER YOU WILL:

➤ Identify and explore your
personal interests

➤ Categorize and estimate
your interests using Holland
Theme Codes

➤ Prioritize your interests
according to your preferences

➤ Match your interests to
potential activities, majors,
occupations, and careers

CHAPTER 3

Understanding Your Interests

Passion?

Interests are the things that you like to do—what inspires, excites and fascinates you. Exploring your interests is important, because understanding your interests can help you define career choices and select a career path you find consistently engaging, one that brings daily excitement to your life. Your interests may include types of work environments, types of people, and types of tasks. Interests may be avocational, leisure activities, or they may be vocational, career-related interests. If you are interested in what you do, you will derive satisfaction from your work. The more you are aware of your own interests and preferences, the better you can match your interests with a satisfying career fit (Montross, et. al, 1995).

My Own Interests and Passions

Take a moment and list ten things in which you are interested or passionate, and explain why. Think broadly. The list may include activities, hobbies, academic subjects, social issues, and other areas.

For example: I love to cook. I find it very gratifying when I use a variety of ingredients to come up with a delicious meal that I can share with someone. It makes me feel proud to display the finished dish to my friends and family.

Now, it's time to create your own list:

1.
2.
3.
4.
5.
6.
7.
8.
9.
10.

What Are Your Passions?

> "In passion, the body and spirit seek expression outside the self . . . the more extreme, the more expressed that passion is, the more unbearable does life seem without it.
> It reminds us that if passion dies or is denied, we are partly dead and that soon, come what may, we will be wholly so."
>
> —*John Boorman.*

Holland's Career Theory

John Holland developed a theory about individuals' interests. He categorized interests into six different theme areas: Realistic, Investigative, Artistic, Social, Enterprising, and Conventional. Typically, one, or a combination of up to three, of these theme areas can characterize a person's interests. Similarly, Holland states that one theme area, or a combination of up to three theme areas, characterizes occupational environments. The combination of interest areas is referred to as a Holland Theme Code. The idea behind this theory is that people search for occupational environments that match their interests. Holland's theory has been used in the development of several vocational interest inventories including the Strong Interest Inventory®, the Self-Directed Search, Kuder Career Search, and Campbell Interest and Skill Survey. *(Prince, 1995)*

It is important to remember that no career assessment can tell you what to do with the "rest of your life." These assessments serve as a guide to highlight trends and potential career interests, but career choice is ultimately your decision based on a combination of factors including values, interests, skills, and personality preferences.

Where Do Your Interests Lead You?

On the next six pages, you will read about each of Holland's occupational themes. Examine Holland's six occupational themes, and decide what areas encompass your strongest interests. For example: If your highest interests are in the Social and Artistic interest categories, you may enjoy creative ways of working with others. Perhaps your high interests involve being around and working with others in collaborative or teaching environments.

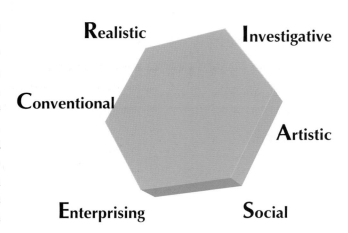

Modified and reproduced by special permission of the Publisher, Consulting Psychologists Press, Inc., Palo Alto, CA 94303 from Strong Interest Inventory® Resource: Strategies for group and individual interpretations in college settings by Jeffrey P. Prince, Reproducible Master 10. Copyright 1995, by Consulting Psychologists Press, Inc. All rights reserved. Further reproduction is prohibited without the Publisher's written consent.

Realistic

Description of Interest Category:

Enjoys hands-on, practical, or outdoor activities. Works well with mechanical and constructive projects. Prefers the concrete and observable over the abstract and implicit. *(Prince, 1995)*

Some typical activities might include:

Using tools that require manual dexterity
Operating, designing, or maintaining equipment and machinery
Doing jobs that produce tangible results

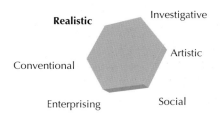

Some skills used might be:

Assembling
Constructing
Supervising
Mechanical
Mathematical
Physical

A person with interests in this category might explore some of these occupations:

R*	Air Force Enlisted Personnel	RSE+	Athletic Director
R	Air Force Officer	RSE*	County Sheriff
R	Bus Driver	RSC*	City or State Employee
R	Correctional Officer	RE*	Baker
R*	Forest Ranger	RE*	Building Contractor
R	Painter	RE+	Professional Athlete
R*	Rancher	RE*	Secret Service Agent
R*	Telephone Technician	REI	Aircraft Sales Representative
R	Union Leader	REI	Environmental Project Manager
R	Computer Technician	REI	Production Manager
RI	Cartographer	REA	Marine Service Manager
RI	Civil Engineer	RES	Animal Trainer
RI*	Machinist	RES	Fire Fighter
RI	Mechanical Engineer	REC	Jeweler
RI+	Navy / Marine Corps Officer	RC	Army Officer
RI*	Petroleum Engineer	RC+	Drafting Technician
RI*	Pilot	RC	Instrument Assembler
RIE	Wine Maker	RCI	Furniture Restorer
RIC*	Navy / Marine Corps Officer	RCI	Software Technician
RIC	Optical Engineer	RCS*	Machine Shop Supervisor
RS*	Industrial Arts Teacher	RCS	Research Assistant
RSI	Customs Agent	RCE	Highway Patrol Officer

(* shows code for men and + shows code for women)

Note: These lists are not exhaustive, but they offer suggestions to help you further explore your career possibilities.

Investigative

Description of Interest Category:

Enjoys analyzing, observing, uncovering new theories, and interpreting data. Often works with ideas in math and science. Prefers flexibility, independence, and values expertise. *(Prince, 1995)*

Some typical activities might include:

Working independently
Solving problems through critical thinking
Doing scientific projects or laboratory research
Collecting and organizing, analyzing and interpreting data

Some skills used might be:

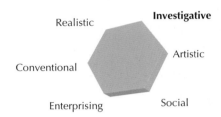

Critical thinking
Computing and technical work
Writing
Compiling
Math/Science
Spatial applications

A person with high interests in this category might explore some of these occupations:

I*	Electronics Designer	IA	Clinical Psychologist
I+	Electronics Technician	IA*	Economist
I*	Internist	IA*	Experimental Psychologist
I	Scientific Researcher	IA+	Inventor
I	Statistician	IA	Language Interpreter
IR*	Animal Science Professor	IA*	Medical Researcher
IR	Astronaut	IAS	Art Appraiser
IR	Chemical / Electrical Engineer	IAS	Counseling Psychologist
IR+	Experimental Psychologist	IAS	Psychiatrist
IR*	Inventor	IS*	Educational Psychologist
IR	Laboratory Technician	ISA	Pediatrician
IR+	Medical Researcher	ISA+	Educational Psychologist
IR	Obstetrician/Pathologist/Surgeon	ISA	Physician Assistant
IRS	Biochemist	ISE	Photographic Engineer
IRS	Geneticist	IER	Project Engineer
IRS	Meteorologist	IER	Laboratory Supervisor
IRE	Archeologist	IEA	Land Surveyor
IRE	Chief Credit Analyst	IEA	Quality Control Director
IRC	Integrated Circuit Layout Designer	IEC	Fire Protection Engineer
IA*	Astronomer	IC*	Computer Operator

(* shows code for men and + shows code for women)

Note: These lists are not exhaustive, but they offer suggestions to help you further explore your career possibilities.

Indiana University Career Development Center

Artistic

Description of Interest Category:

Enjoys self-expression and creativity in themselves or others. Works well in unstructured environments. Often prefers opportunities to write, compose or design. *(Prince, 1995)*

Some typical activities might include:

Composing and writing
Creating artwork (e.g., painting, sculpting, photography)
Working independently
Acting and performing
Playing musical instruments

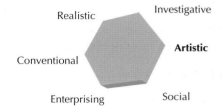

Some skills used might be:

Communication ability
Creativity and imagination
Musical ability
Artistic ability

A person with interests in this category might explore some of these occupations:

A	Art Museum Director	ASE	Playwright
A	Author / Poet	AE+	Ballet Dancer
A	Singer / Entertainer	AE+	Costume Designer
AR*	Landscape Gardener	AE+	Fashion Model
ARI	Model Maker	AE+	Illustrator
ARS	Stage Technician	AER	Amusement Park Entertainer
AI	Anthropologist	AER+	Sculptor
AI+	Landscape Gardener	AEI	Package Designer
AIR	Landscape Architect	AEI	Screen Writer
AIR*	Sculptor	AES	Account Executive
AIS	Orchestra Conductor	AES	Choreographer
AIE	Cryptanalyst	AES	Copy Writer
AIE	Motion Pictures Set Designer	AES	Creative Director
AS*	Music Teacher	AES	Editor
AS	Optical Effects Layout Person	AES	Industrial Designer
ASR	Exhibit Builder	AES	Wedding Consultant
ASI	Dance Therapist	AEC	Photojournalist
ASI	Exhibit Artist		
ASE	Composer		
ASE	Pastry Chef		

(* shows code for men and + shows code for women)

Note: These lists are not exhaustive, but they offer suggestions to help you further explore your career possibilities.

Social

Description of Interest Category:

Enjoys working with people in activities and projects often related to education, counseling or social services. Prefers opportunities to serve and collaborate with others. *(Prince, 1995)*

Some typical activities might include:

Facilitating a team approach
Teaching, training or coaching
Leading discussions
Working on group projects

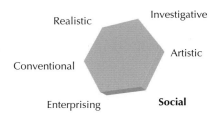

Some skills used might be:

Interpersonal communication
Verbal skills
Empathy
Persuasion
Leadership

A person with high interests in this category might explore some of these occupations:

S	Guidance Counselor	SE*	Football Coach
S	Public Health Nurse	SE*	Juvenile Parole Officer
SRE	Animal Keeper	SE*	Labor Arbitrator
SRE+	Recreation Leader	SE+	Mental Health Worker
SRC	Job Development Specialist	SE*	Recreation Leader
SRC	Mail Carrier	SE+	Vocational Counselor
SI*	Student Personnel Worker	SER	Store / Services Manager
SIR	Orientation Therapist for Persons with Visual Disabilities	SER	Hospital Administrator
		SER	School Superintendent
SIR	Podiatrist	SEI	Radio and TV Producer
SIA	School Psychologist	SEA	Dean of Students
SIE	Correctional Agency Director	SEC	Disk Jockey
SIE	Head Nurse	SEC	Political Scientist
SIE	Medical Records Administrator	SC+	City or State Employee
SIE	Nursing Instructor	SCI	Packaging Engineer
SIE	School Nurse	SCE	Educational Consultant
SA*	Mental Health Worker	SCE	Interpreter for Persons with Hearing Disabilities
SA+	Music Teacher		
SA+	Writer; Children's Books	SCE*	Rehabilitation Counselor
SAE	Food & Drug Inspector		

(* shows code for men and + shows code for women)

Note: These lists are not exhaustive, but they offer suggestions to help you further explore your career possibilities.

Indiana University Career Development Center

Enterprising

Description of Interest Category:

Enjoys influencing and persuading people though leadership, political and promotional activities. Prefers a high level of social impact and interaction. *(Prince, 1995)*

Some typical activities might include:

Selling or purchasing
Managing people and projects
Political involvement
Giving speeches, talks and presentations
Leading committees, groups, organizations and companies

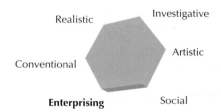

Some skills used might be:

Interpersonal communication
Verbal skills suited to persuading, selling, public speaking and writing
Leadership and development skills

A person with high interests in this category might explore some of these occupations:

E*	Athletic Director	ESR	Financial Planner
E*	Chamber of Commerce Executive	ESR	Museum Director
E+	Foreign Correspondent	ESR	University Business Manager
E*	Funeral Director	ESR	Urban Planner
E+	Personnel Director	ESI	Lifeguard
E	Retailer	ESI	Securities Trader
E*	Sports Reporter	ESA	College Admissions Director
ER*	Nursery Manager	ESA	Head Waiter / Head Waitress
ER*	Professional Athlete	ESA	Lobbyist
ER+	Secret Service Agent	ESC*	Employment Manager
ERI+	Pilot	ESC	Media Director
ERA	Park Superintendent	ESC*	Travel Bureau Manager
ERA+	Stockbroker	EC+	Chamber of Commerce Executive
EIR	Foreign Exchange Trader	EC	Corporation Executive
EIR	Industrial Engineer	EC*	Manufacturer
EIA	Communications Consultant	EC*	Office Manager
EIS	Training and Education Manager	EC*	Stockbroker
EIC	Chief Bank Examiner	EC*	Wholesaler
EA+	Professional Dancer	ECR*	Factory Manager
EAS	Housing Manager	ECR+	Farm Implement Manager
ES+	Occupational Health Nurse	ECR*	Farm Supply Manager
ES*	Personnel Director	ECS*	Auto Sales Dealer
ES+	Sales Manager	ECS+	Funeral Director
ES+	TV Announcer	ECS	Hotel Manager
ESR	Airport Manager	ECS+	Travel Agency Manager

(* shows code for men and + shows code for women)

Note: These lists are not exhaustive, but they offer suggestions to help you further explore your career possibilities.

Conventional

Description of Interest Category:

Enjoys organizing and handling logistics including budget and records. Prefers structure, stability, and efficiency. *(Prince, 1995)*

Some typical activities might include:

Keeping records and financial books
Making charts, graphs and slides
Scheduling, organizing and maintaining office procedures
Writing business reports
Problem solving

Some skills used might be:

Written and verbal communication
Mathematical ability and management of systems and data
Efficiency and organization
Patience

A person with high interests in this category might explore some of these occupations:

C+	Air Force Enlisted Personnel	CSE	Executive Housekeeper
C+	Bank Cashier	CSE	Systems Accountant
C+	Computer Operator	CSE	Title Examiner
C	IRS Tax Auditor	CE+	Baker
C+	Office Manager	CE	Certified Public Accountant
C*	Production Manager	CE+	Courtroom Stenographer
CR*	Army Enlisted Personnel	CE	IRS Agent
CRI	Business Programmer	CE+	Office Worker
CRS+	Army / Marine Corps Personnel	CE+	Pest Controller
CIS	Polygraph Examiner	CE	Tax Preparer
CIE	Building Inspector	CER	Animated Cartoon Painter
CS*	Bank Cashier	CER	Budget Analyst
CS	Surveillance System Monitor	CER*	Dairy Processing Manager
CSI	Financial Analyst	CEI	Customs Inspector
CSE*	County Welfare Worker	CES	Cost Accountant
CSE+	Employment Manager		

(* shows code for men and + shows code for women)

Note: These lists are not exhaustive, but they offer suggestions to help you further explore your career possibilities.

Holland's Theme Codes

Rank your interest areas from 1 to 6:

Realistic   R _____

Investigative   I _____

Artistic   A _____

Social   S _____

Enterprising   E _____

Conventional   C _____

Estimate your Holland Code from your highest area of interest to your third area of interest: Example: EAS

_____   _____   _____

Summary

Identifying your interests can help you to narrow your career options and increase your likelihood of choosing a satisfying career. Identifying them can assist you in selecting a career path you find consistently engaging, one that brings daily enjoyment to your life. We encourage you to use this information to explore academic programs, campus organizations, and occupations that best match your interests.

To further explore your interest areas:

You can further explore your interest areas by considering your involvement in, or attraction to, the following academic majors and programs. In addition, you can consider your interest in your college campus activities and organization memberships. Please review the graphs that follow and try to further identify or confirm your career interests.

Academic Majors and Programs

Realistic:
Agriculture, Ecology, Engineering, Landscape Architecture, Law Enforcement, Military Science, Physical Fitness and Training, Physiology

Conventional:
Accounting, Computer Programming, Mathematics Education, Medical Administration, Office Systems, Small Business Operations, Statistics

Enterprising:
Business Administration, Finance, Government, History, Information Systems Management, International Relations, Management, Marketing, Political Science, Public Administration

Investigative:
Anthropology, Biological Sciences, Chemistry, Computer Science, Criminal Justice, Economics, Geology, Health Sciences, Mathematics, Physics, Psychology, Sociology

Artistic:
Art History, Broadcasting, Classics, Creative Writing, Dance, Design, English, Foreign Languages, Fine Arts, Journalism, Mass Communication, Music Education, Philosophy, Theater, Women's Studies

Social:
Child Development, Counseling, Dietetics, Education, Family Studies, Occupational Therapy, Nursing, Recreation, Religious Studies, Sports Administration, Women's Studies

Note: These lists are not exhaustive, but they offer suggestions to help you further explore your career possibilities.

Campus Activities

Realistic:
Environmental Conservation Organizations, Intramural Sports, ROTC, Sailing Club

Investigative:
Health and Medical Student Associations, Research Laboratory Assistant, Science Associations

Conventional:
Accounting Organization, Mathematics Club, Office Assistant, Secretary/Treasurer of Student Organizations

Artistic:
Film Society, Foreign Language Clubs, Choir, Dance, Band, Student Newspaper, Yearbook, Theater Productions

Social:
Religious Organizations, Residence Hall Advising, Greek Life, Student Union Board, Tutoring

Enterprising:
Business Student Organizations, Campus Political Parties, Orientation Leader, Residence Life, Student Government

Note: These lists are not exhaustive, but they offer suggestions to help you further explore your career possibilities.

Personality Preferences

Exploring Your Uniqueness

By Karen Weist and Daniel Pascoe

IN THIS CHAPTER YOU WILL:

➤ Understand the relevance and meaning of personality preferences and how they relate to career choice

➤ Learn about your personality preferences and their application to choosing careers

➤ Understand and appreciate the diversity and mutual usefulness of different personality preferences

➤ Identify strengths associated with your preferences as they relate to communication

CHAPTER 4
Personality Preferences

Throughout this book you have already explored your values, skills and interests. However, in order to fully evaluate your major and career options, we believe it could be essential for you to explore your personality type. For some people gaining insight to their natural personality preferences and strengths can be crucial to their comfort with making decisions. If you can focus your energy in areas in which you are already naturally gifted you will not have to learn about yourself in retrospect, but rather gain direction to exploring your options.

When you have a greater understanding of what motivates you, then you can make better choices about your major and career, as well as know how to use your natural drives and strengths. By having a better understanding of yourself you can use the strategies that best work for you when adjusting to the ever-changing world around us and identifying areas of personal growth. Learning about your personality preferences could help you to accept yourself for who you are; appreciate what you have to offer; and in the end heighten your career satisfaction (Dunning, 2001). Ultimately, understanding your personality preferences can assist you in clarifying what makes you happy in many facets of your life.

If you have never explored your personality preferences, this chapter can help you learn powerful information about yourself, your preferences and your choices in life. If you are already acquainted with the theory of Personality Type, this chapter could help you to further explore your preferences and consider how these affect your career and personal choices.

Important Note: This chapter is not meant to be a substitute for the actual Myers-Briggs Type Indicator® (MBTI®), but an introduction to personality type and a supplement to the interpretation of your MBTI report. We encourage you to contact your career development center to request the administration and interpretation of the MBTI® by a qualified counselor.

How It All Began

The concept of personality preferences stems from Swiss psychoanalyst Carl Jung's Personality Type theory (Jung, 1921). Although very powerful in content, Jung's writings on this subject were complicated

Exploring Your Uniqueness

"To thine own self be true."

—*William Shakespeare*

for readers without education or experience in psychoanalysis, making it difficult for the general public to understand or apply his classification of different personality types.

In the early 1940s, Katharine Briggs and Isabel Briggs-Myers (mother and daughter) researched Carl Jung's Personality Type theory in the United States to create an instrument that could allow anyone to understand and apply Personality Type theory. They developed the Myers-Briggs Type Indicator® (MBTI) and tested it for over 40 years for statistical reliability and validity, eventually publishing it in the 1970s. Their goal was to help people better understand themselves and others (Myers, 1998).

The Myers-Briggs Type Indicator® is an instrument designed to categorize individual responses to a user-friendly psychological questionnaire into one of 16 different personality types. Each personality type is defined by our unique preferences in four different indicators: our focus of attention, our style of perception, our decision-making style, and our need of order (Myers, 1985). Throughout this chapter you can explore and estimate your preferences for each of these indicators and how they influence your personal choices.

Understanding the Concept of Preferences

To understand the focus of the theory of Personality Type, please try the following exercise:

Write your name in the space provided.

_____

When you are finished, place your pen in your other hand and in the space provided write your name again.

_____

What was different between writing with one hand versus the other? What differences can you identify in your level of comfort, skill, and concentration, or in your speed, outcome, and self-awareness? Using your preferred hand is natural, comfortable and effortless. However, using your other hand is most likely awkward, less skilled, and requires more concentration. You have just experienced a perfect example of a preference. Well, just like handwriting, the Personality Type theory stems from the premise of preferences (Myers, 1998).

More than likely you did not make a conscious choice about which hand you would use to write with today; or if you were asked when you decided to write with one hand versus the other, you might not remember. This is because there are elements of your writing-hand preference which are inborn and thus you do not control. Likewise, some aspects of your personality preferences are inborn and therefore out of your control (Myers, 1998).

Additionally, if something were to happen to the hand with which you naturally write, you could continue functioning. You might even develop skills or an interest in writing with your other hand, thus writing "out of type." Similarly, even though you may have clear personality preferences, often you might choose to behave "out of type." You can even develop a skill or an interest in a preference other than yours. This behavior is normal and does not undermine your preferences (Myers, 1998).

Finally, writing with one hand versus the other does not make you a better or worse person. A writing-hand preference simply makes you different. In the same way your personality preferences are never right or wrong, they are simply different. It is therefore important to remember that personality type classification always refers to healthy diversity (Myers, 1998).

Understanding the Four Indicators

Imagine that a bird flew into your room right now. Think of the pattern of information processing you would follow:

1. First, you might realize that something is flying in your room, thus calling your *attention* to it.

2. Then you might try to *perceive* what it is, whether a threatening object or a non-threatening bird.

3. Third, you might make a *judgment* on its relevance, whether to keep your attention on the bird or move to something else.

4. Finally, you might *order* and store this information in your mind as an example of information processing.

Notice how you more than likely process information through a pattern of attention, perception, judgment and order.

Comparably, your personality is reflected on how you process information, and thus the MBTI® determines your personality type by exploring the combination of your preferences in the following four indicators (Myers, 1985):

1. Energy drive or focus of attention

2. Perception style

3. Decision-making style

4. Need of order

Remember that even though we all have a preference, we can often operate out of our natural preferences or act "out of type." This means that someone with a particular preference can develop skills, or even an interest, in the opposite preference, or vice versa.

First Indicator: Energy Drive or Focus of Attention

Our focus of attention, or our energy drive, determines our first personality preference. We all have a preference for focusing our attention or energizing ourselves either *outwardly* or *inwardly*. The Myers-Briggs Type Indicator® refers to this dichotomy as a preference for Extraversion (*E*) or Introversion (*I*) (Myers, 1985).

Where do you naturally get your energy? Keep in mind that we all can operate out of both preferences, although one comes more naturally. Which is your natural preference?

❏ *E*XTRAVERSION

People who prefer Extraversion like to focus on the outer world of people and activity. They direct their energy and attention outward and receive energy from interacting with people and from taking action.

Characteristics:

Attuned to external environment

Prefer to communicate by talking

Work out ideas by talking them through

Learn best through doing or discussing

Have broad interests

Sociable and expressive

Readily take initiative in work and relationships

❏ *I*NTROVERSION

People who prefer Introversion like to focus on their own inner world of ideas and experiences. They direct their energy and attention inward and receive energy from reflecting on their thoughts, memories, and feelings.

Characteristics:

Drawn to their inner world

Prefer to communicate in writing

Work out ideas by reflecting on memories

Learn best by reflection, mental "practice"

Focus in depth on their interests

Private and contained

Take initiative when the situation or issue is very important to them

---

Second Indicator: Perception Style

The way we perceive things determines our second personality preference. We all have a preference for how we gather information either through *details* and data or possibilities and associations. The Myers-Briggs Type Indicator® refers to this dichotomy as a preference for Sensing (*S*) or Intuition (*N*) (Myers, 1985).

How do you perceive or gather information? Keep in mind that we all can operate out of both preferences, although one comes more naturally. Which is your natural preference?

❏ Sᴇɴsɪɴɢ

People who prefer Sensing like to take in information that is real and tangible—what is actually happening. They are observant about the specifics of what is going on around them and are especially attuned to practical realities.

Characteristics:

Oriented to present realities

Factual and concrete

Focus on what is real and actual

Observe and remember specifics

Build carefully and thoroughly toward conclusions

Understand ideas and theories through practical applications

Trust experience

❏ ɪNᴛᴜɪᴛɪᴏɴ

People who prefer Intuition like to take in information by seeing the big picture, focusing on the relationships and connections between facts. They want to grasp patterns and are especially attuned to seeing new possibilities.

Characteristics:

Oriented to future possibilities

Imaginative and verbally creative

Focus on the patterns and meanings in data

Remember specifics when they relate to a pattern

Move quickly to conclusions, follow hunches

Want to clarify ideas and theories before putting them into practice

Trust inspiration

Third Indicator: Decision-Making Style

The way we make decisions determines our third personality preference. We all have a preference for how we make decisions either based on *logic and analysis* or based on *values and empathy.*

The Myers-Briggs Type Indicator® refers to this dichotomy as a preference for Thinking (*T*) or Feeling (*F*) (Myers, 1985).

How do you make decisions? Keep in mind that we all can operate out of both preferences, although one comes more naturally. Which is your natural preference?

❏ *THINKING*

People who prefer to use Thinking in decision-making like to look at the logical consequences of a choice or action. They want to mentally remove themselves from the situation to examine the pros and cons objectively. They are energized by critiquing and analyzing to identify what's wrong with something, so they can solve the problem. Their goal is to find a standard or principle that will apply in all similar situations.

Characteristics:

Analytical

Use cause-and-effect reasoning

Solve problems with logic

Strive for an objective standard of truth

Reasonable

Can be "tough-minded"

Fair—want everyone treated equally

❏ *FEELING*

People who prefer to use Feeling in decision-making like to consider what is important to them and to others involved. They mentally place themselves into the situation to identify with everyone, so they can make decisions based on their values about honoring people. They are energized by appreciating and supporting others and look for qualities to praise. Their goal is to create harmony and treat each person as a unique individual.

Characteristics:

Empathetic

Guided by personal values

Assess impacts of decisions on people

Strive for harmony and positive interactions

Compassionate

May appear "tender-hearted"

Fair—want everyone treated as an individual

Fourth Indicator: Need of Order

Our need of order determines our fourth personality preference. We all have a preference either for *structure and planning* or for *flexibility and spon-taneity*. The Myers-Briggs Type Indicator® refers to this dichotomy as a preference for Judgment (*J*) or Perception (*P*) (Myers, 1985).

How much structure do you prefer? Keep in mind that we all can operate out of both preferences, although one comes more naturally. Which is your natural preference?

❏ *JUDGING*

People who prefer to use their Judging process in the outer world like to live in a planned, orderly way, seeking to regulate and manage their lives. They want to make decisions, come to closure, and move on. Their lives tend to be structured and organized, and they like to have things settled. Sticking to a plan and schedule is very important to them, and they are energized by getting things done.

Characteristics:

Scheduled

Organize their lives

Systematic

Methodical

Make short-and long-term plans

Like to have things decided

Try to avoid last minute stresses

❏ *PERCEIVING*

People who prefer to use their Perceiving process in the outer world like to live in a flexible, spontaneous way, seeking to experience and understand life, rather than control it. Detailed plans and final decisions feel confining to them; they prefer to stay open to new information and last-minute options. They are energized by their resourcefulness in adapting to the demands of the moment.

Characteristics:

Spontaneous

Flexible

Casual

Open-ended

Adapt, change course

Like things loose and open to change

Feel energized by last-minute pressures

*Modified and reproduced by special permission of the Publisher, Consulting Psychologists Press, Inc., Palo Alto, CA 94303 from **Introduction to Type** 6th Edition, page 10 by Isabel Briggs Myers. Copyright 1998, by Consulting Psychologists Press, Inc. All rights reserved. Further reproduction is prohibited without the Publisher's written consent.*

What is your estimated personality type?

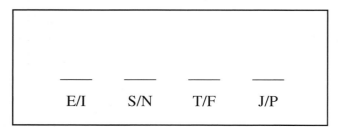

We suggest that you compare your self-estimated type with the reported type you receive once you have completed the MBTI®. Keep in mind that you can disagree with your reported type.

Verifying Type

If estimating your preferences has been difficult for you, please remember that you can and might often operate "out of type." However, you still have a preference, which accommodates you better and makes you more comfortable than its opposite. Remember the handwriting exercise.

You can verify your personality preferences and type by exploring the following:

1. Read carefully your type description and determine whether you identify with the information about your type. Table 5.1 provides brief de-

Indiana University Career Development Center

Table 5.1 Characteristics Frequently Associated with Each Personality Type

	Sensing		Intuitive	
Introversion	**ISTJ** Quiet, serious, earn success by thoroughness and dependability. Practical, matter-of-fact, realistic, and responsible. Decide logically what should be done and work toward it steadily, regardless of distractions. Take pleasure in making everything orderly and organized—their work, their home, their life. Value traditions and loyalty.	**ISFJ** Quiet, friendly, responsible, and conscientious. Committed and steady in meeting their obligations. Thorough, painstaking, and accurate. Loyal, considerate, notice and remember specifics about people who are important to them, concerned with how others feel. Strive to create an orderly and harmonious environment at work and at home.	**INFJ** Seek meaning and connection in ideas, relationships, and material possessions. Want to understand what motivates people and are insightful about others. Conscientious and committed to their firm values. Develop a clear vision about how best to serve the common good. Organized and decisive in implementing their vision.	**INTJ** Have original minds and great drive for implementing their ideas and achieving their goals. Quickly see patterns in external events and develop long-range explanatory perspectives. When committed, organize a job and carry it though. Skeptical and independent, have high standards of competence and performance—for themselves and others.
	ISTP Tolerant and flexible; quiet observers until a problem appears, then act quickly to find workable solutions. Analyze what makes things work and readily get through large amounts of data to isolate the core of practical problems. Interested in cause and effect, organize facts using logical principles, value efficiency.	**ISFP** Quiet, friendly, sensitive, and kind. Enjoy the present moment, what's going on around them. Like to have their own space and to work within their own time frame. Loyal and committed to their values and to people who are important to them. Dislike disagreements and conflicts, do not force their opinions or values on others.	**INFP** Idealistic, loyal to their values and to people who are important to them. Want an external life that is congruent with their values. Curious, quick to see possibilities, can be catalysts for implementing ideas. Seek to understand people and to help them fulfill their potential. Adaptable, flexible, and accepting, unless a value is threatened.	**INTP** Seek to develop logical explanations for everything that interests them. Theoretical and abstract, interested more in ideas than in social interaction. Quiet, contained, flexible, and adaptable. Have unusual ability to focus in depth to solve problems in their area of interest. Skeptical, sometimes critical, always analytical.
Extraversion	**ESTP** Flexible and tolerant, they take a pragmatic approach focused on immediate results. Theories and conceptual explanations bore them—they want to act energetically to solve the problem. Focus on the here-and-now, spontaneous, enjoy each moment that they can be active with others. Enjoy material comforts and style. Learn best through doing.	**ESFP** Outgoing, friendly, and accepting. Exuberant lovers of life, people, and material comforts. Enjoy working with others to make things happen. Bring common sense and a realistic approach to their work, and make work fun. Flexible and spontaneous, adapt readily to new people and environments. Learn best by trying a new skill with other people.	**ENFP** Warmly enthusiastic and imaginative. See life as full of possibilities. Make connections between events and information very quickly, and confidently proceed based on the patterns they see. Want a lot of affirmation from others, and readily give appreciation and support. Spontaneous and flexible, often rely on their ability to improvise and their verbal fluency.	**ENTP** Quick, ingenious, stimulating, alert and outspoken. Resourceful in solving new and challenging problems. Adept at generating conceptual possibilities and then analyzing them strategically. Good at reading other people. Bored by routine, will seldom do the same thing the same way, apt to turn to one new interest after another.
	ESTJ Practical, realistic, matter-of-fact. Decisive, quickly move to implement decisions. Organize projects and people to get things done. Focus on getting results in the most efficient way possible. Take care of routine details. Have a clear set of logical standards, systematically follow them and want others to also. Forceful in implementing their plans.	**ESFJ** Warmhearted, conscientious, and cooperative. Want harmony in their environment, work with determination to establish it. Like to work with others to complete tasks accurately and on time. Loyal, follow through even in small matters. Notice what others need in their day-by-day lives and try to provide it. Want to be appreciated for who they are and for what they contribute.	**ENFJ** Warm, empathetic, responsive, and responsible. Highly attuned to the emotions, needs, and motivations of others. Find potential in everyone, want to help others fulfill their potential. May act as catalysts for individual and group growth. Loyal, responsive to praise and criticism. Sociable, facilitate others in a group, and provide inspiring leadership.	**ENTJ** Frank, decisive, assume leadership readily. Quickly see illogical and inefficient procedures and policies. Develop and implement comprehensive systems to solve organizational problems. Enjoy long-term planning and goal setting. Usually well informed, well read, enjoy expanding their knowledge and passing it on to others. Forceful in presenting their ideas.

scriptions of each type. However, we encourage you to read the descriptions found in the suggested readings, or in your college career library, to gain an in-depth understanding of your type description.

2. Read alternative type descriptions and compare them to yours.

3. Reflect on your past experience and behavior to match it with your type descriptors.

4. Participate in group exercises with people of similar types to further explore your match.

5. Have others who know you well, such as relatives or close friends, give you feedback.

6. Monitor your behavior and its personality type match over time (Myers, 1998).

Another key strategy to verifying your personality type is exploring your "personality functions." Our type is not only the sum of our preferences from the four indicators but also a dynamic relationship between them. It is this unique relationship that distinguishes the 16 personality types. When we refer to "personality function" we are focusing on the middle two preferences: our perception style, **S**ensing or i**N**tuitive, and our decision-making style, **T**hinking or **F**eeling. The combination of these two preferences (**NF, SF, NT** or **ST**) includes a dominant function and an auxiliary function. Each of these functions we display either in our external or internal world, in **E**xtraversion or **I**ntroversion. (A tertiary function and an inferior function also exist, but this chapter will focus on the dominant and auxiliary functions only.) *These concepts are complex. To further understand them refer to suggested readings at the end of this chapter.*

Table 5.2 Priorities of Functions

ISTJ	ISFJ	INFJ	INTJ
Sensing (dominant) — I	Sensing (dominant) — I	Intuition (dominant) — I	Intuition (dominant) — I
Thinking (auxiliary) — E	Feeling (auxiliary) — E	Feeling (auxiliary) — E	Thinking (auxiliary) — E
Feeling (tertiary) — E/I	Thinking (tertiary) — E/I	Thinking (tertiary) — E/I	Feeling (tertiary) — E/I
Intuition (inferior) — E	Intuition (inferior) — E	Sensing (inferior) — E	Sensing (inferior) — E
ISTP	**ISFP**	**INFP**	**INTP**
Thinking (dominant) — I	Feeling (dominant) — I	Feeling (dominant) — I	Thinking (dominant) — I
Sensing (auxiliary) — E	Sensing (auxiliary) — E	Intuition (auxiliary) — E	Intuition (auxiliary) — E
Intuition (tertiary) — E/I	Intuition (tertiary) — E/I	Sensing (tertiary) — E/I	Sensing (tertiary) — E/I
Feeling (inferior) — E	Thinking (inferior) — E	Thinking (inferior) — E	Feeling (inferior) — E
ESTP	**ESFP**	**ENFP**	**ENTP**
Sensing (dominant) — E	Sensing (dominant) — E	Intuition (dominant) — E	Intuition (dominant) — E
Thinking (auxiliary) — I	Feeling (auxiliary) — I	Feeling (auxiliary) — I	Thinking (auxiliary) — I
Feeling (tertiary) — E/I	Thinking (tertiary) — E/I	Thinking (tertiary) — E/I	Feeling (tertiary) — E/I
Intuition (inferior) — I	Intuition (inferior) — I	Sensing (inferior) — I	Sensing (inferior) — I
ESTJ	**ESFJ**	**ENFJ**	**ENTJ**
Thinking (dominant) — E	Feeling (dominant) — E	Feeling (dominant) — E	Thinking (dominant) — E
Sensing (auxiliary) — I	Sensing (auxiliary) — I	Intuition (auxiliary) — I	Intuition (auxiliary) — I
Intuition (tertiary) — E/I	Intuition (tertiary) — E/I	Sensing (tertiary) — E/I	Sensing (tertiary) — E/I
Feeling (inferior) — I	Thinking (inferior) — I	Thinking (inferior) — I	Feeling (inferior) — I

E = Extraverted, I = Introverted, E/I = Theorists differ on the orientation of the tertiary.

If you have a preference for Extraversion, you express your dominant function in outward behavior. If you have a preference for Introversion, you express your dominant function in your internal mental processing. On the other hand, your auxiliary function supports the dominant and is displayed internally if your dominant is displayed externally, and vice-versa. These functions significantly assist us in making choices in life. Find your type in Table 5.2, and consider your dominant function and whether you display this function externally or internally. Then consider your auxiliary function and whether you display this function externally or internally. Do you identify with your dominant and auxiliary functions? To assist you in verifying your personality type, study your type functions in Table 5.2, and try to determine whether they match you.

Using Type in Your Career

Isabel Myers' earliest goal for the MBTI® was to help people choose careers that would match their preferences and personality strengths (Martin, 1995). Once you have estimated your preferences, you can apply what you have learned about the MBTI® and your particular personality type by exploring careers that could make use of your preferences and personality strengths. There have been some notable type-related patterns in career choice. The personality function pairs have significant importance for career selection (see Table 5.3), while your preference on the E/I and J/P indicators are closely related to work satisfaction (Myers 1998).

Myers and McCaulley (1985) stated, "When there is a mismatch between type and occupation, the client usually reports feeling tired and inadequate. According to type theory, the mismatch causes fatigue because it is more tiring to use less-preferred processes. A mismatch also causes discouragement, because despite the greater expenditure of effort, the work product is less likely to show the quality of products that would be developed if the preferred processes were utilized. Tasks that call on preferred and developed processes require less effort for better performance and give more satisfaction."

We caution you not to use personality type as your only basis for career choice. Make sure to include your values, skills, and interests in your decision, and keep in mind that all occupations include and could benefit from a diversity of types. No one type is mutually exclusive to a particular career. As Isabel Myers (1998) indicated, "Each person has access to all eight preferences and . . . many occupations also require the use of all eight, at least some of the time."

Mutual Usefulness of Opposite Types

As you interact with others, you will notice a variety of personality preferences, types, and functions. This diversity of contrasting personality types often presents significant challenges that require strategic team building and collaboration efforts from all members of a group. Once you become aware of your personality type and those of others, you

Table 5.3 Typical Fields of Study or Work by Preference Combinations

ST	SF	NF	NT
Management/business	Health care	Counseling/human services	Law
Accounting/banking	Teaching	Art and music	Physical science
Law enforcement	Religious service	Writing/journalism	Computers
Engineering	Office work	Behavioral science	Management
Skilled trades	Community service	Education	Research

*Modified and reproduced by special permission of the Publisher, Consulting Psychologists Press, Inc., Palo Alto, CA 94303 from **Introduction to Type and College**, page 5 by John K. Ditiberio, Allen L. Hammer. Copyright 1998, by Consulting Psychologists Press, Inc. All rights reserved. Further reproduction is prohibited without the Publisher's written consent.*

Table 5.4 Mutual Usefulness of Opposite Types

Intuitive Types
Can benefit from the natural inclination of Sensing types to
Bring up pertinent facts
Face the realities of the current situation
Apply experience to solving problems
Focus on what needs attention now

Sensing Types
Can benefit from the natural inclination of Intuitive types to
Bring up new possibilities
Anticipate future trends
Apply insight to solving problems
Focus on long-term goals

Feeling Types
Can benefit from the natural inclination of Thinking types to
Analyze consequences and implications
Hold consistently to a policy
Stand firm for important principles
Create rational systems
Be fair

Thinking Types
Can benefit from the natural inclination of Feeling types to
Forecast how others will react and feel
Make needed individual exceptions
Stand firm for human-centered values
Organize people and tasks harmoniously
Appreciate the Thinking type along with everyone else

can explore how opposite types can complement each other. Eventually group and team members can realize that Sensing preferences can complement Intuition preferences and vice-versa, and that Thinking preferences can complement Feeling preferences and vice-versa, in a wide diversity of tasks and activities. Review Table 5.4 to further explore how opposite types can complement each other in most mutual undertakings (Myers, 1998).

Suggested Readings

Dunning, Donna. (2001). *What's Your Type of Career?* Palo Alto: Davies-Black Publishing.

Demarest, Larry. (1997). *Looking at Type in the Workplace.* Palo Alto: Consulting Psychologists Press, Inc.

Ditiberio, John K. and Hammer, Allen L. (1993). *Introduction to Type in College.* Palo Alto: Consulting Psychologists Press, Inc.

Hammer, Allen L. (1993). *Introduction to Type and Careers.* Palo Alto: Consulting Psychologists Press, Inc.

Martin, Charles. (1995). *Looking at Type and Careers.* Palo Alto: Consulting Psychologists Press, Inc.

Tieger, P. D., Barron-Tieger, B. (2001). *Do What You Are.* Boston: Little, Brown, and Company.

TypeLogic: http://www.typelogic.com

Making the Connections

Summary Exercise

By Olivia Martinez and Jeremy Podany

Making the Connections

The chapters preceding this page have allowed you to take some time to evaluate your needs in terms of your values, skills, interests, and personality preferences. You have explored your decision-making style and have realized that a systematic approach is the best way to narrow your choices. By now you have begun to reflect on your values in regards to how they fit a work environment, identifying at least five that you consider as essential in your work life. We have worked to assist you in discovering your skills through a few reflective exercises. You have identified a list of interests that are important to you that will play a key role in determining what you want to spend your time doing in your career. And finally, you have explored your personality preferences and have identified some occupations that will help you begin exploring a good fit. During the course of your life, you will continue to re-evaluate these needs, and as you have different experiences, your needs will change, and you will have a greater understanding of your self-concept. The exercise in this section will allow you to see how your values, interests, skills, and personality preferences come together to determine a good fit in the occupation of your choice.

> **"Writing fiction has developed in me a sense of where to look for the threads, how to follow, how to connect, find in the thick of the tangle what clear line persists. The strands are all there . . ."**
>
> —*Eudora Welty*

Making the connections between your career components and the career options you are considering will help you narrow your options and find a good fit. It is essential that you thoroughly understand all that will be expected of you in your career choice. You may find that one of the careers you are considering does not match your own values, skills, or interests. This may be difficult for you to realize, but it is best to come to this understanding now rather than later. The next couple of chapters in this book will guide you through the process of researching specific informa-

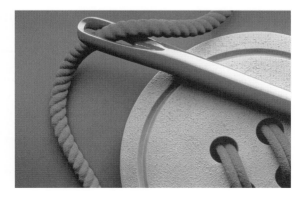

tion on the careers you are considering. This particular piece of the process is especially helpful.

Exercise

Choose an occupation you are considering and complete the following exercise. Use the books in your library to find descriptions or the on-line sources provided by your career counselor or instructor. The following resource is especially helpful and easy to use: (Occupational Outlook Handbook (2002). Electronic Version: http://stats.bls.gov/oco/ocoiab.htm)

Directions: Write the name of an occupation you are considering as a career goal. Estimate the work values a person in this career would have according to their job tasks. Use the same description to list the skills that will be used in this position. Assign a Holland Theme Code and MBTI® type and to this occupation based on the description given in career books. Be sure to pay close attention to the reasons that you are assigning a personality type and Holland code to this particular occupation. Finally, justify your estimates by giving reasons for each code, type, skill, and value.

Title of Occupation: _____

Values (Use Work Values List):

_____   _____   _____

_____   _____   _____

Reasons: _____

_____

_____

Skills (Use the Skills list from the skills chapter in this book or the Skillscan Profile™):

_____   _____   _____

_____   _____   _____

Reasons: _____

_____

_____

Exercise

Holland Theme Code (Use the descriptions of interests for Holland Theme Codes from Chapter 3 or the Strong Interest Inventory):

(RIASEC)   _____   _____   _____

Letter Codes   **Reasons:**

_____   _____

                    _____

_____   _____

                    _____

_____   _____

                    _____

MBTI (Use the MBTI type letters from Chapter 4):

_____   _____   _____   _____

E or I   S or N   T or F   J or P

Reasons:

E or I _____   _____

                     _____

S or N _____   _____

                     _____

T or F _____   _____

                     _____

J or P _____   _____

                     _____

Exercise

In the box below, list your own values, skills, interests, and personality preferences. Refer to chapters 1-4 in this book to fill in the information below. After filling out the textbox with your personal information, write a summary below the box that describes you best.

For Example: I enjoy working with others, helping others, instructing, and guiding. I enjoy creative ways of helping others and solving problems. I am good at the following things: reading, organizing events, drawing, singing, sports. I like activities that involve teams and sports. I enjoy art in the form of music and crafts. I gain my energy from others and take in information through my senses. I like gathering the details and prefer that information is given to me in chronological order. I make decisions based on how it will affect the people around me. I enjoy planning ahead and try to be organized in everything I do.

My Personal Career Profile:

My Work Values: _____ _____ _____
                _____ _____ _____

My Skills: _____ _____ _____
           _____ _____ _____

My Holland Theme Code (Interests): _____ _____ _____

My Personality Preferences (MBTI): _____ _____ _____ _____

Personal Summary:

_____

_____

_____

_____

_____

_____

_____

E x e r c i s e

Compare the career components of the career you researched with your own profile. List the reasons why your career components (values, skills, interests, and personality preferences) align with your career goal. What areas do not align well and why?

My Potential Career Goal (Title of Occupation):

_____

_____

Reasons why my personal career components align with my potential career goal:

_____

_____

_____

_____

_____

Areas that do not align well with my potential career goal:

_____

_____

_____

_____

_____

_____

PART II

Exploring Options:

What's Out There?

Career Exploration Process

SELF-INFORMATION

Self-Concept
Values
Skills
Interests
Personality Style
Decision-Making Style

EDUCATIONAL INFORMATION

Majors/Minors
Concentrations
Prerequisites for Admission
Course Requirements
Experiential Education
Campus and Community Resources

WORLD OF WORK INFORMATION

Types of Jobs
Nature of Work
Work Environments
Educational Requirements
Skill Requirements
Employment Outlook

C
A
R
E
E
R

Choosing Your Major Route

Don't Let Choosing a Major Become a Road Block

By Sue Sgambelluri and Jennifer DeSana

IN THIS CHAPTER YOU WILL:

➤ Decode all the different ways that your college or university organizes academic programs (and figure out what this all means for *you*)

➤ Identify academic options at your school

➤ Explore some creative ways of combining these options to better meet your needs

➤ Research majors and what they can offer you

➤ Use your self-information to identify majors that are the best fit with your goals

CHAPTER 5

Choosing Your Major Route

Celebrity Major Match

Can you correctly match the major to the celebrity?

1. ____ Al Gore	A.	Psychology
2. ____ Amy Tan	B.	American Studies
3. ____ Bill Clinton	C.	Music
4. ____ Bill Cosby	D.	Economics
5. ____ Brooke Shields	E.	Law
6. ____ David Schwimmer	F.	Physics
7. ____ Ghandi	G.	Philosophy
8. ____ Glenn Close	H.	Chemistry
9. ____ James Cameron	I.	Speech/Theatre Arts
10. ____ Jane Pauley	J.	Government
11. ____ Janet Reno	K.	Anthropology/Theatre
12. ____ Lisa Kudrow	L.	Sociology
13. ____ Maria Shriver	M.	English
14. ____ Martin Luther King, Jr.	N.	Fine Arts
15. ____ Mick Jagger	O.	Physical Education
16. ____ Patrick Ewing	P.	Biology
17. ____ Paul Reiser	Q.	International Studies
18. ____ Sandra Bullock	R.	English Literature
19. ____ Sharon Stone	S.	Writing/Fine Arts
20. ____ Steve Martin	T.	French
21. ____ Tommy Lee Jones	U.	Drama

Answers: 1.J, 2.M, 3.Q, 4.O, 5.T, 6.L, 7.E, 8.K, 9.F, 10.A, 11.H, 12.P, 13.B, 14.L, 15.D, 16.N, 17.C, 18.U, 19.S, 20.G, 21.R

Adapted from Kristen Lindsay, University of Toledo.

Don't Let Choosing a Major Become a Road Block

Who would think that these majors could lead to the careers they did? Steve Martin a Philosophy major? Bill Cosby a Physical Education major? As we'll talk about throughout this book, your major is only a *part* of your career path . . . but it is an important part. It's worth your time and effort to check out all your options and find the best fit with your needs and goals. In this chapter, we'll help you do the following:

- **Decode** all the different ways that your college or university organizes academic programs and figure out what that means for you.

- **Identify** the academic options at *your* school.

- **Explore** some creative ways of combining these options to better meet your needs.

- **Research** majors and what they can offer you.

- **Use** your self-information to identify majors that are the best fit with your goals.

Learning to Read the Map

Very often, the process of choosing your academic program is difficult because of the complex and often confusing relationships between different programs and different divisions of the same college or university. Choosing your academic path requires that you have a working knowledge of your college or university, its program offerings, and how they're organized within the institution.

Why is this so important? Simple. As an exploratory student, your job is to gather information. The quality of the information you gather on majors and other academic programs depends on your ability to identify the best sources of information. For example, a general advisor may be a great help when you register for basic prerequisite courses. That same advisor may be of limited assistance, however, when you need to learn about internship requirements for a specific major. Take time now to learn about your institution and the best sources of information beginning with the "vocabulary words" below.

Universities, Colleges, Schools

Generally, a university will be divided into several separate schools (sometimes called colleges). For example, a large comprehensive university with a wide range of course offerings may have any or all of the following schools or colleges:

- College of Liberal Arts and Sciences

- School of Education

- School of Engineering and Technology

- School of Nursing

- College of Business (or Commerce and Finance)

- School of Agriculture

- School of Health and Family Sciences

- School of Music

- School of Public and Environmental Affairs

- School of Science

- School of Library and Information Sciences

- School of Communications

Each of these schools (or colleges) will then be further divided into departments. For example, a college of liberal arts may be divided into separate departments for anthropology, English, folklore, criminal justice, political science, sociology, modern languages, and theater. A school of engineering may be divided into separate departments for mechanical engineering, electrical engineering, nuclear engineering, and chemical engineering. A school of business may be divided into separate departments for accounting, marketing, human resource management, and finance.

Majors, Minors, Concentrations, and Certificates

Requirements for a bachelor's degree in a given major will generally include 30 to 40 separate courses (approximately one third of which are major credits) and may also include an internship or some practical experience. Your courses may be housed in several departments or even several different schools, but they will generally involve a focus in one department. Advanced (400-level and 500-level) courses will be required, as will in-depth research, field work, or training.

At times, single- or even double-majoring may still not allow you to meet your personal or professional goals, because your interests are so specialized. Toward that end, many colleges and universities offer an individualized major program. For example, you may have a strong interest in theatrical set design and want to prepare for a career in that field. If your institution does not offer that specific major, you may be able to work closely with a faculty member to pick courses in engineering and theater that meet your specialized needs.

Many departments also offer minors in selected fields. Completing a minor may only require six or seven courses in a given department, but it *will* provide you with a basic overview of the field and some exposure to advanced concepts and skills.

Finally, some departments may offer concentrations or certificate programs in selected areas. These programs allow a department to formally recognize the completion of core coursework or a certain level of skill or proficiency. Often this concentration or certificate may be required for an individual to become licensed to practice a given trade or profession. Teachers' certification and foreign language proficiency programs are two examples.

Any or all of these options—majors, minors, concentrations, and certificates—may be available through your college or university. Talk with advisors to learn about academic programs and how they are organized at your institution.

Is Picking a Major the Same as Choosing a Career?

Most programs of study allow you to develop the skills, interests, and specialized knowledge required to be successful. For some academic programs, the connection between classroom learning and a specific career is clear and direct. For other programs, this connection isn't quite as clear.

Direct Relationships

Some majors relate directly to a career. Typically, the course work here clearly relates to that job and you'll get the training, licensure, or certification required by law.

MAJOR	CAREER
Accounting ——▶	Accountant
Athletic Training ——▶	Athletic Trainer
Education ——▶	Teacher

Indirect Relationships

Most majors, however, do not relate directly to one career. That is, a major can lead to a variety of careers depending on your interests, skills, experiences, activities, and values. A career counselor or advisor can help you identify options like these:

MAJOR	CAREERS
History ——▶	Attorney
	Journalist
	Museum Curator
	Foreign Service Officer
	Secondary Teacher
	Investment Banker or Stock Analyst

MAJOR	CAREERS
Psychology ——▶	Advertising Executive
	Counselor
	Human Resource Administrator
	Probation Officer
	Health Care Professional
	Marketing Researcher

Ways to Add to Your Academic Package: Minors and Concentrations

At most schools, you will be able to combine your major with another major, with minors, or with concentrations and certificates to meet your personal and professional goals. A business student interested in pharmaceutical sales may take some core science courses to learn about the major activities in that industry. A psychology student wishing to serve as a therapist in a specific geographic area may become fluent in Spanish, Chinese, or Russian. A journalism student hoping to report on corporate negotiations and takeovers may want to complete a minor in business.

Choosing your major simply because you have heard that you are "guaranteed a job" can leave you frustrated and disappointed once you actually get into the classes. *By choosing a major that really interests you, you increase your chances of doing well academically and finding a career that satisfies you.*

> While the job search for students selecting an "indirect major" will be different (and maybe a bit more labor intensive) than that of students choosing a "direct major," professional careers are available for both alternatives. Regardless of your choice, you will always need to think seriously about the minors and concentrations you pursue as well as the activities, internships, and volunteer experiences that build your skills and enhance your marketability.

Your Final Destination: Developing Your "Short List" of Majors

The journey of a thousand miles begins with a single step. In a similar way, choosing your major begins with simply narrowing your choices to five or six subjects or majors based on your values, skills, interests, and goals. You've already assembled a lot of the self-information needed for this task through your work in earlier chapters. Now, this chapter—and this section—gives you a chance to apply this information.

The Tour Guide: Obtaining the List of Majors

All but the most specialized schools offer a variety of majors with a variety of admission requirements and potential career paths. While the list below is a pretty comprehensive starting point, be sure to obtain an up-to-date official listing of majors available at *your* college or university.

Accounting	Audiology
Advertising	Banking and Finance
Afro-American Studies	Biochemistry
Agriculture	Biology
Agronomy	Botany
Animal Science	Broadcasting
Anthropology	Business Administration
Archaeology	Chemical Engineering
Architecture	Chemistry
Art and Design	Civil Engineering
Astronomy	Classics
Athletic Training	Clothing and Textiles

Communications	Medical Technology
Computer Science	Metallurgy
Criminal Justice	Meteorology
Dance	Microbiology
Drafting	Mining Engineering
Economics	Music
Education	Nuclear Physics
Electrical Engineering	Nursing
Engineering	Occupational Therapy
English	Oceanography
Environmental Science	Pharmacy
Finance	Philosophy
Fire Science	Photography
Folklore	Physical Education
Food Science and Nutrition	Physics
Foreign Languages	Political Science
Forestry	Psychology
Genetics	Public Administration
Geography	Public Policy
Geology	Public Relations
Geophysics	Purchasing
Health	Real Estate
History	Recreation
Home Economics	Religion/Theology
Horticulture	Retail Management
Hotel/Restaurant Mgmt.	Social Work
Human Resource Mgmt.	Sociology
Industrial/Labor Relations	Speech Pathology
Insurance	Sports Marketing
Interior Design	Statistics
Journalism	Telecommunications
Library Science	Theater and Cinema
Literature	Transportation
Marine Science	Urban Administration
Marketing	Urban Planning
Mathematics	Veterinary Medicine
Mechanical Engineering	Zoology

Quite a menu, isn't it? Sorting through a list like this using your own self-information may seem like a huge task at first. If so, it might be helpful to revisit the exercises you completed earlier and summarize the three or four points from each one that will help you rule out (or rule in) majors from the above list.

Researching Majors and Other Academic Programs

Armed with your "short list" of possible majors, you are now ready for more in-depth research using a number of campus resources and some very specific questions.

Sources of Information

Just as we all have different personality traits, many of us may also have different learning styles and preferred sources of information. Any or all of the following strategies may be helpful to you as you research the majors on your "short list."

- Read your college or university publications and Web sites, course catalogs, degree requirements, and advising guidelines.

- Discuss your possible majors with a variety of people. Departmental faculty, academic advisors, admissions representatives, current students, and program graduates can all be great sources of information.

- Test drive your top majors by taking a 100-200 level class or two classes in each major. While you probably would not want to rule out a major based on your experience in a 100-level class, you may get a better sense of the subject and the faculty in the department if you explore upper level courses.

- Get experience in the career field or major through paid part-time work, job shadowing, internships, student organizations, or volunteer activities.

- Attend information sessions and other programs for the departments that you are considering. Meet the faculty and advisors and explore some of the issues below with them.

- Visit web sites that will help you become more familiar with this major and with related majors. Start with the following and consider other links that might be recommended by the department:

  http://www.indiana.edu/~udiv/majors/
  Indiana University's Majors and Careers Series

  http://www.career.fsu.edu/ccis/matchmajor/matchmenu.html
  Match Menu Sheets

  http://career.utk.edu/students/majors/majorsindex.asp
  What can I do with this major?

http://www.udel.edu/CSC/mrk.html
Major Resource Kits

http://www.uncwil.edu/stuaff/career/Majors/
What Can I Do With A Major In . . . ?

http://myroad.com
College Planning and Career Planning

Questions to Ask: The Major Choice Checklist

Once you have identified the best sources of information on an academic program, your next task is to develop a *good list of questions* that will get you detailed, informative answers. Very often, students are tempted to ask simply, "What can I do with a major in _____?" Keep in mind, however, that *any* major can—in theory—lead to *any* career. Take time to dig deeper using the following questions:

- Where have graduates of this program gone? What specific organizations have hired them and what do their career paths look like? Then ask yourself, do these career paths seem like a good fit with your own needs and goals?

- What are the prerequisites for admission to this school? To this department? To this major? Do any of these units require a minimum GPA for admission? What is the admissions process?

- What courses and experiences are required to complete this major? Are there any internship or practicum requirements?

- Of the courses you have taken to date, which will apply toward this major? Toward general graduation requirements? What further coursework will be required?

- What skills and expertise will you develop through this major?

- What kinds of time or financial requirements are a part of this academic program? (For example, a music major will require many hours of practice time. An interior design major will require a financial investment in the tools and materials for the profession.)

- What might I dislike about this major?

Light at the End of the Tunnel?

As you work through the research process outlined above, please keep two things in mind. The degree to which you like your major and enjoy your classes is perhaps the best single predictor of how well you'll do academically. And how well you do during your college experience can be one of the best single predictors of your success in the world of work.

If you have explored and given careful thought to your own goals and the majors you have identified, have confidence in your choice! Look forward to participating in the many student organizations and pre-professional activities that will prepare you to begin your career.

| **E x e r c i s e** | **RESEARCHING MAJORS** |

Your Goals

➤ To identify the people and offices that will be most helpful as you gather information about your academic options.

➤ To ask good, useful questions and get a clear picture of what it really means to pursue a particular major.

The Project

Getting a clear picture of what a major requires can demand a lot of research on your part. Working as a group will let you cover more ground faster and, for that reason, you'll be working with a few classmates to tackle this project. While we expect that work will be distributed fairly among all group members, it is entirely up to your group to decide how best to divide responsibilities.

Using the questions below as a starting point, talk with advisors, students, faculty, staff, and alumni about what it means to be in this particular major. Ultimately, your group will present your findings to the class and field questions about this major. While you won't be required to submit a written report, you will need to submit an outline of your presentation to your instructor prior to the presentation. Your group must discuss the key points listed below.

Questions

Prerequisites—Are certain courses required *before* you can be admitted to this major? Is a minimum GPA needed? What kind of application process is required? How competitive is admission to this major?

Course Requirements—What courses are required to complete this major? How much variety and flexibility will you find in these requirements? Are all courses concentrated in one department or are they spread across several departments? Do courses tend to be theory-based, "practical," or a balance of both?

Projects and Assignments—What kinds of projects and assignments are typical in this major? (For example, will you be working independently on problem sets or will you be collaborating with groups to design and present marketing plans?) Based on the course requirements you identified above, what are some *specific* examples of major projects and assignments? Are there any "tools of the trade" that you will be using frequently in this major (e.g. software, lab equipment, etc.)?

Special Requirements—Does this major place any unusual or distinctive demands on your time or resources? (For example, a music performance major requires many hours of practice time in addition to class time. An interior design major may require you to purchase expensive equipment and materials.) Just how much time, travel, or money is involved?

Questions
(continued)

Getting Experience—What kinds of internships, practicum experiences, volunteer work, or other out-of-classroom experiences are required (or recommended) in this major? What kinds of experiences are desirable? How do you go about finding these experiences? Are you "on your own" or will you find help from the department?

Fellow Students—In general, how might you describe the students in this major? What are they like? What kinds of interests and values do they tend to have in common? Are there any student organizations or pre-professional associations in this major? What types of students would be well-suited for this major? Why?

Faculty and Staff—How does your group define "high quality faculty and staff"? To what extent do the faculty and staff associated with this major meet those standards? How helpful and available are these advisors, faculty members, and administrators?

The Future—Where specifically have graduates of this program gone? What jobs do they hold and what career paths have they followed?

Resources

This project requires that your group interview at least one departmental advisor for this major (not a generalist advisor), at least one instructor (graduate instructor or professor), and at least one currently enrolled senior in this major. Please list their names and contact information on the cover sheet for your outline.

In addition, you're encouraged to talk with a variety of people who can shed light on the major. Alumni are an especially good resource as are other students, advising specialists, and internship coordinators.

Reminders

Even more important than the *amount* of information you gather is the *quality* of that information. Be sure to seek out individuals who are well-informed and who can be at least somewhat objective in their analysis. Be a "critical consumer!" Look for inconsistencies or outright differences in what you hear from those you interview, and ask for clarification when you need to. Good Luck!

On a separate sheet, prepare an outline of your group presentation that covers the points outlined in the research questions above. Include a section summarizing the most helpful sources of information and any remaining questions that you have. See the sample outlines on the following pages for an overall format.

Exercise

RESEARCHING MAJORS COVER SHEET

Major: _____

Group Members: _____

_____

_____

Advisor Name: _____ Title: _____

Dept.:_____

Office address: _____

Time and date of interview: _____

Phone: _____ E-mail address: _____

Instructor Name: _____

Dept.:_____

Office address: _____

Time and date of interview: _____

Phone: _____ E-mail address: _____

Student Name: _____

Address: _____

Time and date of interview: _____

Phone: _____ E-mail address: _____

Additional
Contacts (Optional): List these on a separate sheet using the format above.

Sample Outline

Researching Majors Presentation Outline

I. **Prerequisites**
   A. Courses
   B. GPA Requirements
   C. Application Process
      1. Forms
      2. Personal Statements
      3. Interviews

II. **Course Requirements**
   A. Distribution Requirements
   B. Major Courses
   C. Electives
   D. Overall Comments on Course Content, Variety, and Flexibility

III. **Projects and Assignments**
   A. Major Papers/Projects
   B. Research Requirements
   C. Major Lab Work
   D. Overall Comments on Projects and Assignments

IV. **Special Requirements**
   A. Time
   B. Costs—e.g., Materials and Equipment

V. **Getting Experience**
   A. Part-time Jobs
   B. Internships
   C. Volunteer Work/Activities
      1. Campus
      2. Community

VI. **Fellow Students**
   A. Numbers
   B. Typical Interests, Values, and Personality Traits
   C. Student Organizations

VII. **Faculty and Staff**
   A. Research Interests
   B. Reputation, Ranking

VIII. **The Future**
   A. *Possible* Career Paths and Related Requirements
   B. *Actual* Career Paths—A Sampling of Alumni
   C. Additional Education
      Advanced Degrees
      Specialized Training

IX. **Suggestions for Further Research**
   A. Most Helpful Sources
   B. Least Helpful Sources

Note: This is just a sample outline! Depending on the major you research, your own outline may eliminate some of these points and add others.

LINKING SELF INFORMATION WITH MAJOR CHOICES

Now that you're armed with solid information about yourself, your task is to *research* majors that interest you and *assess* how well each one "fits" you and your needs. This assignment will give you an opportunity to do just that.

First, choose a specific major that interests you and that you wish to research. Next, use a variety of materials from academic departments, your career resource center, or your local library to review prerequisites, course requirements, student characteristics, major projects, and other important aspects of this major. Based on this information, indicate whether you accept or reject this major. In either case, *you must justify your decision* using information you have gathered about *yourself* and about the *major*. Read through the questions below and respond to them on a separate sheet of paper using specific examples of your own personal qualities, skills, values, and interests.

Important:

When you respond to the questions below, be sure to focus on the <u>MAJOR</u> you have chosen and NOT the careers to which the major may lead. For example, think about what it would be like to *major* in accounting for the next four years—not about what it would mean to *be* an accountant. Note that the examples below are not meant to be copied, but to help you begin thinking about the information you gather.

Questions:

1. Review your <u>Values Assessment</u>. Consider your top two or three values and assess how well this <u>major</u> can meet your needs. In what ways would this major <u>not</u> meet your needs?

   (e.g.: "My values assessment indicated that I have a very high need for prestige and for mental challenge, and I don't think that majoring in _____ will give me either of those things. I'll always have to explain to people exactly what the major means and the classes just don't seem very challenging.")

   (e.g.: "My values assessment indicated that I place great importance on interpersonal relations and on leadership. Majoring in_____ would probably meet these needs very well, since most of the classes will require group projects and collaboration. These groups could provide me opportunities to build working relationships and to develop my leadership skills.")

Exercise

2. Take a look at your <u>Skills Assessment</u> and the <u>transferable skills list</u>, and review your strengths and areas of improvement. In what ways will this major suit you and the skills you currently have? What skills might you need to develop further in order to be successful in this program? Give examples of courses and projects that illustrate your points.

> (e.g.: "I already have pretty strong communication skills, but I really hope to strengthen my administrative skills. Majoring in _____ should let me do that, particularly through courses in _____ and _____.")

3. Refer back to your Holland Themes. In what ways does this major match your <u>INTERESTS</u> as they are reflected in your Holland Theme Code? In what ways does it fail to do so? Once again, give specific examples of classes or projects that illustrate your points.

> (e.g.: "Majoring in apparel merchandising ties in with my interest in sales and marketing and also with my creative interest in art. Classes I will be taking in these specific areas include _____, _____, and _____.")

4. Now, review the results of your *Myers-Briggs Type Indicator* and decide how well this major "fits" your personality. For example, will pursuing this major make good use of your preferences? Your preferred approach to solving problems? Will the class work allow you the degree of structure (or freedom) that you prefer? Give specific examples of classes and projects that illustrate your points.

> (e.g.: "Majoring in math would require a great deal of attention to detail and focus on standard approaches to problem solving. As a sensing type, I believe I would feel very comfortable in this major, but I might not develop my Intuitive qualities as much as I'd like to while in college.")

> (e.g.: "Majoring in journalism would require that I adhere to strict deadlines for assignments, but it would also require that I be flexible and respond quickly to late-breaking stories on campus when I did class projects. My Judging and Perceiving scores were tied, and I feel that the balance between the two will allow me to be successful in this major.")

5. Finally, indicate whether or not you will accept this major, and summarize the four or five points that most influenced your decision.

6. What *additional* types of information would have helped make this decision easier for you?

Gathering Good Information

Researching Careers

By Jan Van Dyke and Karen Weist

IN THIS CHAPTER YOU WILL:

➤ Identify resources that will help you research a variety of career fields that match your interests, values, skills, and personality type

➤ Learn how to get hands-on experience and try out a career field of interest to you

➤ Understand the importance of field research, internships, job shadowing, and volunteering

CHAPTER 6

Gathering Good Information

A fter completing the self-assessment section, you now have a better sense of who you are and what you want. As you begin to research career fields, reflect back on your assessment results. As you read the information about careers, ask yourself these questions: How does the career field match my values? My interests? My skills? My personality style? My talents? In addition, your assessment results have given you some career titles that you may want to research. Perhaps you have known what you wanted to be since the age of five, but do you know what the job's requirements are? Do you know the job market, the realities of day-to-day work in the position, or what degree it requires? Or perhaps you are still feeling completely lost about the right job for you. The resources described in this chapter will help you gather good information to answer your questions.

This chapter will review different resources that you can use when researching a variety of different career fields. We will discuss printed and electronic resources, as well as experiential opportunities to research careers. There are also exercises that will give you an opportunity to practice researching careers.

Career Research with Print and Electronic Resources

The print and electronic resources mentioned below are available to you in public libraries, college libraries, and career centers. It is important for you to get to know your reference librarians and career center staff. These people can be of great assistance to you in finding the specific career information that you are seeking.

Occupational Outlook Handbook

A great place to start your career exploration is by using the *Occupational Outlook Handbook*. This handbook provides you with career information on over 250 jobs. It is updated every two years by the U.S. Department of Labor. It is also available on the Web at: www.bls.gov/oco/. The *Occupational Outlook Handbook* provides you with many details about each job including: training and education required, earnings, working conditions, skills needed,

Researching Careers

"**Nothing has such power to broaden the mind as the ability to investigate systematically**"

—*Marcus Aurelius, Meditations*

advancement opportunities, projected job growth, and sources of additional information including Web sites.

O*NET

The *O*Net Dictionary of Occupational Titles* gives detailed descriptions of 1,094 occupations covering about 99% of the workforce in the United States. This resource is available in directory format, and a similar format is available on-line from the U.S. Department of Labor. The Web site is: http://on-line.onetcenter.org/main.html.

Encyclopedia of Careers and Vocational Guidance

This very comprehensive career resource is available as a four-volume set. This directory provides similar information that is also provided by the *Occupational Outlook Handbook*. Job titles and career fields are listed in alphabetical order in the table of contents.

Occupational Outlook Quarterly

This publication is published by the U.S. Department of Labor's Bureau of Labor Statistics. This magazine lists a variety of different career fields in the table of contents. The articles provide up-to-date information about each career field listed in each edition. The *Occupational Outlook Quarterly* also has many very helpful articles regarding the future job outlook for many different career fields.

Vocational Biographies Series

This series provides career information for hundreds of jobs, including an informational interview for each career field that is cited. Job titles are listed under each career field. It is a collection of interviews with people talking about real jobs. You don't have to go to the trouble of setting up the informational interview—the logistics and interview are already done for you. This is an excellent resource for researching very specific jobs. Examples include: Jingle Writer, Compulsive Gambling Counselor, Stunt Coordinator/Performer, Interpreter/Translator for the Deaf, and Dolphin Trainer. The Vocational Biographies Series is often available in your college or university career center.

College and University Career Centers

Check with your college or university career center. It may have a very extensive collection of career books, videos, CD's, and career information files. The following are examples of books that have been written as part of a career information series: *Great Jobs for Economics Majors,* and *Great Jobs for Computer Science Majors* (published by VGM Career Horizons). The following book titles are examples of another career information series: *Careers For Good Samaritans and Other Humanitarian Types, Career For Financial Mavens and Other Money Movers,* and *Careers for Nature Lovers and Other Outdoor Types* (published by VGM Career Horizons).

Career Opportunities in Education and *Career Opportunities in Art* are examples of books in the *Career Opportunities in* series published by Facts on File. *Careers in Health Care* and *Careers in Marketing* are part of the VGM Professional Careers Series. *Opportunities in Occupational Therapy Careers* and *Opportunities in Mental Health Careers* are examples of books in the *Opportunities in* career series published by VGM Career Horizons. An additional series also published by VGM Career Horizons is the *Real People Working in* career series. Examples of this career series include: *Real People Working in Sales and Marketing* and *Real People Working in Business.*

Career books concerning special career topics include: *The American Almanac of Jobs and Salaries, The Work at Home Sourcebook, Kiplinger's Working for Yourself, The Best Jobs For The 21st Century, International Jobs: Where They Are, How to Get Them,* and *The Global Resume and CV Guide.*

Ask your reference librarian or career center staff about these book series.

Web Sites

Look at your college's career center Web site. Many career center Web sites have links to other Web sites that can help you research careers, professional associations, and job listings.

Career Information Files

Many college career centers and public libraries have developed files containing career information about a wide variety of career fields. This information may include career and job descriptions, training and educational requirements, future job outlook, and salary ranges for a variety of career fields. This type of information may also be obtained from the Internet or professional associations.

Career Information on Video, CD, DVD

Check with your college or university career center for information that can be in a variety of formats including video, DVD, and CD. This information can include videotaped interviews from professionals representing a variety of career fields. Career and company information is also available in CD format.

Computerized Career Information Systems

Computer programs such as SIGI PLUS, DISCOVER or FOCUS can assist you in exploring your interests, values, skills, and personality and in applying this information to possible majors and careers. These computer programs are also available to assist you with researching careers and majors that interest you.

Professional Associations

State, regional, and national professional associations are valuable sources for a variety of career information. Through them you can learn about certification requirements, job leads, internships, educational opportunities, career and job descriptions, and more. Attending association conferences, conventions, and/or meetings will give you the

opportunity to network and possibly set up information interviews with association members.

A good place to start researching professional associations is using the directory entitled the *Encyclopedia of Associations* which can often be found in a career center or the reference section of a library. Another way to locate contact information for professional associations is to use the *Directory of Associations'* Web site: http://www.vcanet.org/vca/assns.htm.

Another excellent resource to use when looking for professional associations is the Internet. Do a keyword search using the name of the career field you are interested in, for example "clinical psychology." This will lead you to various sites on that subject and will often include professional associations for that career field.

If you have found a Web site of a professional association in a career field you are interested in pursuing, then you may have found all of the information you wanted. If not, you can email, write, or call the membership department or the public information office of the association, and ask them for the information you are seeking. The following are some suggestions for questions you could ask:

- Could you please send me membership information?

- Do you have a student rate for joining your association?

- Do you have a brochure that describes your association?

- Could I have a sample copy of your association's newsletter or journal?

- What are the dates and locations of future national, state, or regional conferences and/or conventions?

- Do you have a brochure describing careers in the field of_____?

- Does your association provide placement services for its members?

- Is your association aware of non-paid or paid internships in your career field? If so, would you send me a list?

- Do you have a Web site on the Internet?

- Can you send me a price list of your publications?

- Is your association aware of financial aid or scholarships available in this career field? If this information is available, would you send me a list?

- Does your association have a list of colleges/universities that would offer further training in this career field?

Some examples of professional associations include:

- American Marketing Association (AMA) www.ama.org

- American Psychological Association (APA) www.apa.org

- National Association of Social Workers (NASW) www.naswdc.org

---

Food for Thought

Treat every experience as an opportunity to explore career fields of interest to you.

Chambers of Commerce

Your local chamber of commerce has contact information for a variety of businesses and organizations. The chamber of commerce, public library, or career center may have a collection of chamber of commerce directories that can be very helpful when researching possible internship and job shadowing opportunities within your community.

Periodicals

Check with your library or career center to see what career magazines or periodicals are available. The titles of some of these periodicals include: *Job Choices, The Black Collegian, Hispanic Business, Hobsons Career Guide, Diversity: Career Opportunities and Insights.* These career magazines will have articles about a variety of career fields. Articles in the magazines often include current information on: future career trends, future job outlook, salary information, educational requirements, and career descriptions.

Additional College and University Resources

Check with your college or university career center for directories and Web sites about other colleges and universities throughout the United States. Students who are identifying majors or looking ahead to obtaining an advanced degree can find valuable information in these materials. Advanced degrees and professional schools may include: law school, medical school, and various graduate school programs. Books that can be helpful to students identifying majors include: *The College Board Index of Majors and Graduate Degrees, The College Majors Handbook, College Majors and Careers, Majors Exploration: A Search and Find Guide for College and Career Direction.*

Career Research Based On Experiential Learning

Getting hands-on experience is often cited as the most valuable tool to making a career decision. Whether conducting an informational interview (field research interview), spending a day job shadowing or working as an intern, the key to successful career exploration is variety. The more job settings you visit, the more comfortable you will become with your career decisions. The following options can help you explore careers, gain experience before you graduate, and can help you build some important contacts (network) as you search for a good match.

Career Fairs/Job Fairs

The career center at your university or college is a good place to research the time and location of various career fairs or job fairs. These fairs are an excellent opportunity for you to meet employers representing a broad range of career fields. Representatives from a broad range of companies, federal government agencies, and non-profit organizations will have information tables and will be happy to provide you with brochures, flyers, and Web sites concerning career information, and job descriptions in their specific organization. They may also help you locate job leads and internship opportunities.

Field Research/Informational Interviewing

Talking with professionals about their career is a valuable source of information. You can gain insights from people who have made career decisions, obtained the required education and who are working in a career field of interest to you. This is called **Field Research or Informational Interviewing.** You are encouraged to contact a professional in a career of interest and gather as much information as possible on that career. To conduct field research, follow the guidelines described below.

The field research interview is an excellent way to check what you have only thought about, read, and heard. The in-person interview can offer information that is:

- Current

- Specific and related to local situations

- Personal and subjective

- Reflective of the "on-the-job" atmosphere

It takes time to identify, contact, arrange, prepare for, and interview with a professional. You should get started right away!

Why Conduct Field Research/Informational Interviews?

Consider these specific advantages of an informational interview:

1. It allows you to acquire specific first-hand information on a particular career.

2. It allows you to obtain information about a company, an occupation, or an industry.

3. It helps you decide on a career path, especially if you are uncertain. You can learn more about a variety of occupations.

4. It pinpoints industries that are booming during difficult economic times.

5. It helps you become adept at professional interaction.

6. It increases your self-confidence when dealing with people.

7. It enlarges your circle of professional contacts.

How Does a Field Research Interview Compare with a Job-Hunting Interview?

As in a job-hunting interview, a field research interview is a two-way conversation. However, it is generally more relaxed and informal. The field research interview occurs in a context of extraordinary freedom and control. You define its focus and structure, and conduct it entirely for your benefit. You decide what information is needed. Your questions should reflect what you really want to learn.

Who Should You Interview?

Essentially, target individuals who hold positions you would like to explore. Do not assume that potential employers are your only sources for quality information. Look for individuals who:

- Share a common interest, enthusiasm, or involvement in some activity or lifestyle that appeals to you.

- Work in settings you like (e.g., hospitals, politics, large corporations, theater).

- Work in career areas in which you are interested (e.g., broadcaster, stockbroker, criminal lawyer, market researcher).

- Work in specific jobs in specific organizations (e.g., a newscaster in a local radio station, a stockbroker at Merrill Lynch, a criminal lawyer in a legal aid office, or a market researcher at IBM).

Where Do I Find These People?

The most obvious individuals include friends, family, and neighbors. You will also want to contact faculty advisors and your instructor to generate potential contacts. Additional sources might include the university alumni database, professional associations, and community service agencies (American Management Association, Chamber of Commerce, United Way, etc.). You can also use the yellow pages of phone books and staff listings on organizations' Web sites.

Are you looking for concrete information about a particular field or company? If so, then go to two kinds of people: those "insiders" who know you well enough to be candid, and strangers who will inevitably give more of a public relations talk but may possess a broader perspective than your company "pal."

Are you looking for an insight into the future direction of an industry? If so, then go to a recognized industry expert. Are you hoping that the information will be helpful in identifying additional people to interview? If so, then go to those who are well-connected and can lead you to others.

People are generally interested in talking about what they do and how they do it. In fact, you may have some ideas that will be of interest to them. However, do not waste their time. If you do a little research on the company first, and prepare a list of questions in advance, you should be able to complete an informational interview in 20 to 30 minutes. Be prepared, and leave within appropriate time limits.

Preparation? Do Your Library Research First!

Know exactly what kind of information you want. Generally, do not ask something routine that is readily available elsewhere. Know your own interests, skills, values, and how they relate to the person you are interviewing. Know as much as you can about the organization for which the interviewee works as well as the industry in which it operates. We have included questions that will help you conduct your interview. Be familiar with the questions you want to ask. If you are prepared with your questions and have done some initial research, you will be more relaxed and confident about this interview. You also have the opportunity to make a lasting impression. Some students have received internships by making a good impression during these in-person interviews.

How Do I Initiate Contact?

Contact the person by phone and identify yourself by name and purpose of your call. Explain to the person that you would like to meet him or her to learn about his or her occupation. Emphasize that this is a career that you are considering pursuing. If the person is not able to do the interview with you, thank him or her and ask if he or she knows anyone else who may be able to help you. If you are having problems arranging an interview for your field research, talk to your instructor or a career counselor.

Job Shadowing

Job shadowing a professional is a great opportunity to learn about careers and work settings that exist in real life, not in a textbook. Job shadowing is essentially an extended form of field research. When you job shadow a professional you can spend a day—or a couple of hours—watching them work. You will gain a clearer picture of the current working conditions and challenges faced by the professionals in that field. You are encouraged to shadow a variety of professionals in your field of interest to expand your knowledge of that career field.

Observing someone at work may sound intimidating, but do not let fear keep you from exploring your career options. Most working professionals welcome the opportunity to show college students real-life working conditions. Setting up a day of job shadowing is as easy as making a phone call. Visit the career center to speak to a career counselor, ask an academic advisor or professor, connect with an alumnus, or simply open the phone book to find contacts. Academic departments and career centers routinely organize job-shadowing events.

To get the most out of your day of job shadowing, you will want to do some basic research by using some of the resources mentioned earlier in this chapter. Try to learn some of the basic jargon or educational requirements needed to work in the profession. Ask questions while you job shadow. As a matter of fact, you should consider conducting an informational interview during your job shadowing. Don't hesitate to pitch in if you're asked to, but remain sensitive to the schedule and workload of the person you are shadowing. At times it may be necessary to fade into the background. It is always important to be conscious of your professional behavior—you want to make a positive impression. This may also be a perfect opportunity to start building a list of contacts (network) for future references and potential opportunities.

Career-Related Volunteering

There are many career advantages gained by working as a volunteer. Volunteering is a good way to experience many careers without making a huge time commitment. In some cases, you may be able to do the specific job that interests you. For jobs that require more education or training, you might be able to volunteer in a related job that still exposes you to your career interests. For example, if you're interested in being a doctor, contact your local hospital and see if you can volunteer in the emergency room. The volunteer opportunity may only be 2 or 3 hours a week; however, you can learn a tremendous amount about a career field in a very short time.

Many colleges have lists of volunteer opportunities. Check with the career center or student activities office and their Web sites. The local newspaper or community center also posts volunteer opportunities.

Part-time and Full-time Jobs

Jobs can teach you a considerable amount about your interests and help you develop skills useful for any career while earning money for tuition and living expenses. An added bonus to working is gaining experience to help you build a career path.

For example, if you want to pursue a career in education, consider interviewing with someone in the local school system. While you may not have the education or experience to land a teaching position, you can still apply your skills to other positions like a teacher's aide or tutor. You can develop your skills while you achieve your academic goals. Combining work and education will help you solidify the career choices in your life. Many part-time jobs do not require extensive training or skills to get started. You may be able to work part-time while enrolled in college. Studies show that working 8 to 10 hours a week during an academic semester can have a positive impact on academic performance.

If you are thinking about looking for a part-time job during college or a full-time summer job, talk

---

Food for Thought

98% of employers use experiential education programs (internships) to recruit for future workforces. *Job Outlook*, NACE, 2000

with your professors, instructors, or advisors about possible jobs that fit your academic major and career goals. You should also be able to find part-time job listings with the student employment office on your campus.

Internships

Internships are structured experiences that not only allow you to test-drive a career field but will also provide you with an opportunity to gain relevant work experience. This type of exploration will offer you the most in-depth information about a career field and is typically related to your career or academic goals. Internships are a great way to integrate academic course work into practice. In some cases, you can even earn academic credit. Internships can be paid or unpaid, full- or part-time, and range in length from a few weeks to an entire semester, summer, or academic year depending on your goals and the employer's needs. During your internship, you can expect to assume some responsibility for projects, similar to an entry-level professional in the field, while still being under the supervision of a professional. Most students find the experience they gain from an internship to be the most valuable in their career decision-making process. An increas-

ing number of students, including freshmen and sophomores, are participating in internships, many are even doing two or three internships during their academic career.

How do you find an internship? Your college career center can be a great resource for finding internship opportunities. Academic departments, professors, parents, friends, and alumni are valuable resources as well. An internship search is similar to a job search and generally requires a resume and cover letter. You do not necessarily need a great deal of experience to get an internship, but previous part-time work and/or campus involvement is very beneficial.

Exercise

FIELD RESEARCH/INFORMATIONAL INTERVIEW

Field Research is valuable for career networking, gaining confidence, and finding out about the realities of the world of work while in an academic program.

1. Prior to the interview:

  a. Decide on a career field that interests you and choose an individual to interview.

  b. Research (per page 88).

  c. Contact the individual, introduce yourself, request an informational interview, and describe briefly what you would like to learn from this interview.

  d. Establish a date, time frame (20 to 30 minutes) and place for the meeting.

2. During the interview:

  a. Introduce yourself and review the purpose and goals of your interview. (It is not to get a job.)

  b. Ask at least two questions from each section, A through F, of the Field Research/Informational Interview Questions on the following pages. Feel free to phrase questions in your own words. Be selective in the questions you want to ask your interviewee. Only ask questions that are of interest to you. Listen carefully to what the person is saying. He/she may answer one of the questions you have planned to ask later on. It is all right to have your questions written down and in front of you as you speak to the person, yet be familiar with what you want to ask.

  c. Take notes regarding the answers to your questions.

  d. Ask for a business card to ensure that you obtain correct information regarding the person's name and title for a thank-you note and other future follow-up.

3. After the interview:

  a. Send a brief thank-you note to the person you interviewed. If the tone of the interview and your interactions were generally easy-going and casual, a handwritten note or e-mail is fine. If your interactions were more formal, then type and mail your thank-you note.

  b. Document your interview in a paper.

    1. Create a cover page providing:

      • Name of professional interviewed

      • Position/Title

      • Organization's name and address

      • Your name and class section

    2. Type the questions and answers from the interview.

    3. Write a 1-page summary statement about your experience and "new" thoughts about this career.

Exercise

FIELD RESEARCH/INFORMATIONAL INTERVIEW QUESTIONS

If you need help thinking of questions to ask, here are a few to get you started until questions of your own come to mind. Use only those questions that genuinely interest you and that are pertinent to the career you are researching.

A. Occupational Environment

1. How would you describe the environment in which you work?

2. Describe a typical day at work (e.g., your routine or duties you perform on a regular basis).

3. How much flexibility are you allowed on your job in terms of dress, hours, vacation, etc.?

4. Are you made aware of supervisory expectations?

    Do these expectations seem realistic to you?

    Are you allowed any input in defining your goals?

5. How independent can you be on this job?

6. What portion of your job involves interacting with others such as co-workers and/or the public?

7. How much "outside" or overtime work is required on your job (e.g., weekends, nights, etc.)? What does this work involve?

B. Occupational Requirements and Experience

1. What college courses were most helpful to you in your preparation for this career?

2. What types of tools or equipment, if any, are necessary to perform your job?

3. Is special certification, licensing, or an advanced degree necessary to perform your job?

4. What personal qualities and skills do you see as important for success in this occupation?

5. Is travel involved in your job? If so, how much and what type?

6. How much job relocation is expected or needed to advance in this career?

C. Benefits and Frustrations

1. What are the major rewards of your job?

2. What are the major frustrations you encounter on your job? How do you deal with these frustrations?

3. What fringe benefits are offered on your job?

4. What personal benefits to your career does this job provide?

5. What is the salary range for entry-level positions in this occupation? What do the salary trends look like for the future?

Indiana University Career Development Center

D. Personal Views

1. How did you, personally, get interested in this area of work?

2. What was your undergraduate field of study?

3. Did you have any practical experience or training, other than college, prior to your current job (e.g., part-time jobs, internships, volunteer experiences)?

4. How did you get your current job?

E. Outlook

1. What are the opportunities for advancement in this field?

2. What is the current demand for people in this occupation?

3. Do you foresee any changes in this demand in the future?

4. How is the field likely to be affected by technological changes?

F. Advice

1. If you were in charge of hiring someone in your line of work, what criteria would you use to make your selection?

2. Are there any professional groups that I, as an undergraduate, can join which would be beneficial to me?

3. Do you know of any other people in this field who might be willing to talk with me about their experiences?

Note: The questions you ask, and the way you ask them, will depend on the information you seek from your interview and the tone of the interview. Some questions are more appropriate than others, depending on the situation, the person, and the organization.

Evaluating Your Findings

Write a one-page summary of your findings. Include the following information:

• Is there a "good fit" between your self-information and the career requirements, or are there differences?

• If there are differences, how much of a problem will those differences be for you working in that career?

• Will they be significant enough to make you unhappy or unsatisfied in your profession, or are they minor sacrifices you are willing to make for an occupation you enjoy?

In Part III of this book, you will have the opportunity to continue examining work environments and the types of interactions you may encounter.

PART III

Taking Action:

How Can You Move Forward?

Career Exploration Process

SELF-INFORMATION

Self-Concept
Values
Skills
Interests
Personality Style
Decision-Making Style

EDUCATIONAL INFORMATION

Majors/Minors
Concentrations
Prerequisites for Admission
Course Requirements
Experiential Education
Campus and Community Resources

WORLD OF WORK INFORMATION

Types of Jobs
Nature of Work
Work Environments
Educational Requirements
Skill Requirements
Employment Outlook

C
A
R
E
E
R

Making Career Decisions

A Journey of Learning

By Marianna Savoca and Elena Polenova

IN THIS CHAPTER YOU WILL:

➤ Recognize fear as a barrier to making decisions

➤ Learn that career decisions are a series of mini-decisions

➤ Identify different decision-making styles

➤ Learn about a seven-step technique for making decisions

CHAPTER 7

Making Career Decisions

According to the *American Heritage Dictionary*, a decision is the passing of judgment on an issue under consideration. You have learned about the process of career development and defined some of what you know about yourself by completing the exercises in the last chapter. Surely it must now be easy to make the biggest, most important, far-reaching decision of your life; that is, what career will you choose that will satisfy you for the rest of your years?

Sounds scary, huh? Intimidating? What if you make the wrong decision? Are you doomed for all eternity?

In reality, we make decisions all the time. Some are easy; we don't think about them much at all:

- *"I think I'll leave for school an hour early this morning so I can study for my exam."*

- *"I'm going to join the debate club to improve my public speaking skills."*

  Some decisions are more complex, and, therefore, may seem larger, have greater risk, and require more time and consideration:

- *"Should I pursue the study abroad option or a summer internship?"*

- *"Do I move to New York after graduation?"*

- *"Do I accept the job that pays more, or the job that I know I'll love?"*

Before making a career-related decision, you must first be willing to decide. You must be open to "passing judgment on an issue of consideration." The issues under consideration in this case relate to your life plans.

The purpose of this chapter is to teach you about career decisions—what factors may influence these decisions, how they are made, how often they are made, and what value you may derive from each career-related decision you make—starting now. One of the common myths of the career development process is the belief that this is a one-way road, with no turns or stops, and the destination should be known at the starting point. This mental picture creates the legitimate fear that if you take a wrong turn at the beginning, it can ruin the whole journey. A primary barrier that prevents people from making career-related decisions is **FEAR**. Fear may take different forms.

A Journey of Learning

> **"By making choices we learn to profit from our mistakes. Waiting for the perfect choice is to miss it all."**
>
> —*Alexandra Stoddard*

Fears as Barriers

FEAR OF MAKING A LIFE DECISION: You are so overwhelmed by the sheer enormity of the decision before you that you simply don't know how to begin: *"How can I decide what I'm going to do for the rest of my life? If I'm only 19, does that mean what I decide today will be what I do for the next 50 years?"*

FEAR OF MAKING A BAD CHOICE: You believe that a mistake now means complete failure. *"If I choose to major in biology and don't get accepted into medical school, my whole college career would be a waste."*

FEAR OF DISAPPOINTING OTHERS: You are concerned that your decision will not meet the expectations of someone important to you (like a parent or family member). *"My father is sending me to college so I can become a lawyer and work for his firm someday. How can I tell him that my passion is to become an archaeologist?"*

FEAR OF COMMITMENT: You may be concerned that a decision now would limit your opportunities. *"I'd like to keep all my options open, just in case something interesting pops up."*

FEAR OF THE UNKNOWN: You might think, *"How can I decide if I have no idea what's out there?"*

The Winding Road

Let's imagine that you decide to relocate from Lafayette, Indiana to a warmer climate. Can you decide immediately where you will be happy? Probably not, unless you had heard about a wonderful place which you incorporated into your dream. Where will you go?

First, you decide on the state, then which part of the state, then the city or region. You do your research—you read books, browse the Internet, watch videos, talk to people. Let's say that you settle on South Carolina. You then make another decision—to get into the car and drive there, and see it first for yourself.

Your tank is full of gas. You have no deadline, but you want to arrive sooner rather than later. Obviously you should not go to Canada first, but even if you do, this won't be the end of the world. As soon as you realize that you are heading north (it's getting cold), you can make a U-turn. This will delay you, but maybe you will see something unique and beautiful that will enhance your life experience.

You are now headed in the right direction. At every junction, you must make another decision. Do you want to take the fenced-in toll road, or take a scenic drive and enjoy the view at the expense of speed? Do you stop for coffee? If you do, you may find yourself engaged in exciting conversations with local people that may ultimately change you in some way. Do you take a small detour and see some attractions that you probably would not see otherwise? Do you get eight hours sleep each night and arrive in South Carolina full of energy, or do you drive 16 hours per day to get there as soon as possible? What if you are suddenly struck with the beauty of the Smokey Mountains and decide to go to Tennessee instead of South Carolina? You can definitely do so, because you are the master of your own destiny, and you can make your own choices.

Is it clear that throughout this journey, you make several mini-decisions that affect the outcome of the larger journey? With each decision, you acquire more knowledge, make your best effort to digest this knowledge, and then use it in planning your next move.

The process of career development is in fact a series of *mini-decisions*; each will move you ahead on your career journey. Considering smaller decisions helps you overcome your fears of taking the first step. What major to choose? Is a minor necessary? What electives to take? Should I take a class that does not relate directly to my major but sounds interesting? Should I go directly to graduate school, or is a bachelor's degree enough? Should I study abroad? What internship to take—the one that pays the most, or the one where future employment is most promising? How are my work values prioritized: money, challenge, interesting job, good benefits, or any combination of those?

Each of these decisions requires thinking and research within your own decision-making style.

It is doubtful that one decision-making model or strategy will work perfectly for every person, nor will any single model account for the complexities of each person's values, emotions, experience, and decision factors. However, we must begin somewhere—the basics are always a good starting point.

Decision-Making Styles

Two psychologists, Lillian Dinklage and Norman Sprinthall, coined these terms to describe some common decision making strategies:

LEAPING LENA
An impulsive, spur-of-the-moment decision-maker. Lena primarily uses her intuition and feeling to guide her decision-making process.

AGNES AGONIZER
Weighs the pros and cons of each decision without actually making the decision. Agnes is afraid of making the wrong choice.

MAURIE MORATORIUM
Avoids making a decision at all. Maurie hopes that by postponing action, the situation will resolve itself somehow.

INEZ INNER HARMONY
Makes "feel good" decisions.

FREDDIE FATER
Removes himself from the responsibility of making a decision and uses fate as his excuse. Freddie claims that since fate is at work, his decisions make no difference.

HERMANN HYPNOTIZEE
Prefers to allow others who know better to make his decisions (parents, advisors, friends).

PENELOPE PLANNER
Approaches decisions rationally, and weighs pros and cons like Agnes, but is confident in her abilities to make a good decision based on objective measures, and takes action to do so.

Exercise

1 Describe a decision you recently made which you perceived to have a negative result:

_____

_____

_____

_____

Which character, or combinations of characters, best reflects the style you used to make this decision? Elaborate.

_____

_____

_____

_____

2 Describe a different decision you recently made which you perceived to have a positive outcome:

_____

_____

_____

_____

Which character, or combinations of characters, best reflects the style you used to make this decision? Elaborate.

_____

_____

_____

_____

Reflecting on both these examples, what have learned about your personal decision-making style?

_____

_____

_____

_____

These exercises demonstrate that elements of each personal style are acceptable considerations when making decisions. In fact, you may have incorporated more than one style in your examples. This is okay, however, we recommend the systematic approach used by Penelope as the starting point for your decision journey.

DECIDES

Psychologists Krumboltz and Hamel (1999) developed a seven-step systematic technique, called **DECIDES**:

DEFINE THE PROBLEM AS SPECIFICALLY AS POSSIBLE. Remember that your big life decisions can be broken down into smaller, more manageable mini-decisions. An example of poor problem definition: to choose a satisfying career. Better problem definition: By the end of this semester, I will narrow down major and career options to those that best match my interests, skills, and values.

ESTABLISH AN ACTION PLAN, WITH SPECIFIC DEADLINES. For example, you may read your bulletin and specific course descriptions, and speak to advisors before the registration period begins.

CLARIFY VALUES. What is really important to you? You completed a values exercise in Chapter 1 to identify things of value to you as they relate to work—e.g., income, prestige, security. If you would like to become an actor, are you willing to risk low pay and an irregular work schedule? Or perhaps you yearn for the prestige and salary of a top investment banker, yet are you willing to adjust your lifestyle to accommodate a 90-hour workweek?

IDENTIFY ALTERNATIVES. You may be able to think creatively and brainstorm options on your own. However, this is an opportune time for you to work with a career advisor, who likely has resources to assist you.

DISCOVER PROBABLE OUTCOMES. Can you reasonably predict outcomes of each alternative generated? For example, if you wish to become a physician, you'll go on to medical school, then residency of approximately 8 years before establishing your own practice. To pursue an academic career in the humanities, you will likely relocate several times.

ELIMINATE ALTERNATIVES SYSTEMATICALLY. Compare alternatives to your values, interests, and skills. For example, you might consider a double major in computer science and biochemistry, yet pursuing such a rigorous program would not give you time to also join the intramural basketball team and/or have an active social life. Are you the type to sacrifice social life for study time?

START ACTION! Clearly doing something to pursue your goals is preferred to sitting back and waiting for your career to happen to you.

> **If you are concerned that this approach is too rigid for your style, remember that these are guidelines—the elements are key, not the order.**

Factors to Consider: Lifestyle & Passion
By Arlene Hill

"Nothing great has been and nothing great can be accomplished without passion" —Hegel

"Although Freud said happiness is composed of love and work, reality often forces us to choose love or work" —Pogrebin

Loving what you do does not guarantee a fulfilling career. In addition to the assessment work you have done so far, you still need to evaluate how your skills, values, interests, and personality fit with your lifestyle goals. You need to compare your dreams to your career reality. At the same time, you need to pay attention to your passion; what will you compromise, and what will you fight to achieve?

When Dreams and Reality Collide

We receive many messages throughout our lives about what careers we should pursue: *Look at that arm—you are going to pitch for the Yankees someday.... She's so smart—we know she's going to become a doctor.... With a voice like that, he'll make it on Broadway. She's the next Marie Curie.... Everyone in this family has been a great teacher.* Sometimes the messages are the daydreams we have about what our lives will be like: *In my ideal job, I will set my own hours, teach poor children how to read, and make $50,000 a year. I am going to spend my life designing sailboats and racing in the America's Cup.*

Eventually, we start to examine the reality of these messages. Throughout high school and college, the level of competence and competition of our peers rises and may exceed our own; our interests wane or we learn new skills.

Sorting through these messages can be a difficult task: *I do well in science, but I really like computers better. I know I'm smart enough to be a doctor, but I like being creative and designing web pages. While it would be nice to help people, I'm not sure if I want to devote the next 8 years of my life to studying medicine when I don't know if I'll really like it. I don't really like sick people. Am I crazy? Doctors are well respected and they make a ton of money. Who would want to become a web designer instead of a doctor?*

In this case, there is a conflict between interest and skills. When you know you are good at something, it can be difficult to give it up, particularly for an interest that you haven't explored fully. In the example above, the "bird in the hand" of becoming a doctor is appealing because it offers safety and security, as there is no guarantee that the "two birds in the bush" of becoming a web designer will necessarily be achievable or enjoyable.

The key to solving these types of situations is to fully explore and understand the options before making a choice. Rather than having to give up the known of becoming a doctor for the unknown of becoming a web designer (what a tough choice!), this person should learn more about becoming a web designer, and test the field by doing an informational interview, taking classes, and trying an internship or shadowing a professional. The decision then becomes one of choosing between two known commodities—a much more effective decision.

Sofia's Dilemma: A Real Life Example

Sofia is a freshman at Stony Brook University, Long Island, NY. Her strong subjects in high school were math and physics. She is confused about how to choose a major, and whether that also means she should choose a career. She heard that quantitative skills are good for business and that business pays well. What exactly does that mean? What skills? What business? And how well exactly does it pay?

Sofia visited the Career Center and found a dazzling array of career opportunities for students of math and physics: actuary, researcher in a national lab, university professor, computer programmer, teacher, Wall Street analyst, veterinarian, and financial advisor. She also discovered a broad range of salaries and years of training required. Sofia was overwhelmed by all this information. When her career advisor asked her if she also had considered applied math and economics, she felt faint. Fortunately, she had taken economics in high school and hated it, so she turned that down easily. But applied math? Is it different from "plain" math and how? To what does it apply?

HERE ARE SOME OF THE MINI-DECISIONS THAT SOFIA MADE:

1. She ruled out economics on the basis of her previous experience (she disliked it).

2. She read the Applied Math section of the University Bulletin, including description of major, classes, and faculty specializations. This sounded intriguing enough for her to decide to take the first statistics course next term.

3. After studying the requirements for the math major, she felt less confident that she could do well in the 300-level classes. She decided to give it one more try and enrolled in the 200-level course.

4. After speaking with the physics advisor, she learned that this major involves many labs. She recalled that she was not fond of this type of hands-on science. She also didn't feel like she blended well with the crowd at the physics department and decided not to pursue physics.

EPILOGUE: At the end of the following semester, Sofia learned that she really loved statistics; she felt that formulas came alive when applied to real-life problems. Meanwhile, the 200-level math class required a lot of effort, and though she did reasonably well, she was not particularly excited about climbing to a higher level. Her mini-decisions allowed her to confidently choose Applied Math & Statistics as her major.

Exercise: Can you identify elements of DECIDES in Sofia's example? (e.g., She *established* her action plan with a career advisor.) What others do you see?

_____

_____

_____

Consider this point a rest stop on Sofia's career journey. Sofia no longer feels faint—she is energized and ready to continue with new decisions—exploring potential career paths, internships, an academic minor, etc.

As you have seen through Sofia's situation, any effort you make will bring benefits sooner or later and will move you closer to your destination. You may think that this affirmation is too tidy. You're thinking about the decision you made that yielded a negative result, and others like it. What about that class you failed? You have undoubtedly taken a science course—either in high school or in college. Do you remember that a negative result in a scientific experiment is just as useful as a positive one? The experiment is conducted to confirm or deny a hypothesis. Results allow the scientist to develop a new hypothesis and proceed from there. Results of your career decisions allow you to move forward with new information, similar to the process of the scientist.

Changing Directions is OK!

For example, Ian always dreamed of becoming a medical doctor. During his freshman year, he set aside five hours per week to volunteer at the local hospital. After a few weeks, having witnessed patients suffering and seeing the tremendous responsibilities placed on doctors, Ian felt that the stress of such a career would be too much for him to bear. He decided that rather than pursue medical school, he would apply his skills in science, his interest in the medical field, and his desire to help people, to a career in pharmacology, where he would be involved in the creation of new drugs that would ultimately help patients.

Exercise: Ian's learning was a direct result of testing out a potential career path; he also never expected that a negative result (i.e., not liking hospital work) could lead him to a positive outcome. Think of a decision you made which yielded a negative outcome: _____

_____

_____

What did you learn from this experience?

_____

_____

_____

Learning may not always be that intentional. Jessica, a sophomore, needed a part-time job. She started working at a local fast-food restaurant. She wasn't happy taking orders at the counter, or putting hamburgers together. She was frustrated with what she believed were inefficient procedures. Jessica mentioned to her manager that she had ideas to improve things. Her manager was so impressed with her observations and suggestions, that she was promoted to a supervisory position. Jessica excelled at this role and discovered that she really enjoyed managing people and processes—this part-time job experience resulted in her choosing a career in management.

> "Mistakes are the portals to discovery."
>
> —James Joyce

Both examples show that actions, regardless of outcomes, produce results that can lead to new decisions and new actions. This process leads to real success if you are able to stay focused and positive—interpreting learning experiences throughout your journey. Are you inspired? You're now ready to face big life decisions head on! Think about your upcoming career decisions—and use the knowledge gained in this chapter to address them.

Setting Goals and Moving Forward

By Paul Timmins and Arlene Hill

IN THIS CHAPTER YOU WILL:

➤ Begin to consider career goals

➤ Learn to create and assess achievable, challenging, and measurable goals

➤ Develop a set of semester-long goals and action plans

Setting Goals and Moving Forward

For a moment, think about all the work that it took you to enroll in college. Even if you always knew that you'd be attending your current college, you still had to successfully complete high school, complete the application forms, figure out how you'd pay your tuition, and begin your new life in college. Or maybe your process was more extensive. Maybe you considered several colleges, read through the piles of college brochures, made some campus visits, applied to several schools, got accepted by some, and decided which one to attend. Whatever steps you undertook to make your choice and to get to where you are today, one thing is clear: whether or not you ever thought of it in these terms, you had a clear goal in mind—to enroll in college. It was a fairly significant goal, and there were a lot of small actions you had to complete to make it happen.

Goals are statements about our commitment to achieve something we value, and they can be short-term or long-term. Having a clear goal gives us a sense of purpose and drives us to succeed. It helps us to focus our actions, to set priorities, and to evaluate our accomplishments. But sometimes, big goals can be intimidating. Since we can't achieve them all at once, it can be tough to get started. Upon closer examination, these big goals are really long-term goals composed of many short-term goals. How did you feel when you started thinking about going to college? Confused? Scared? Excited? To achieve the long-term goal of choosing a college, you first had to set a short-term goal of choosing the colleges to which you would apply. The next short-term goal was to complete the application forms, and so on. Moreover, choosing a college may have been a short-term goal toward reaching your longer-term goal of obtaining a bachelor's degree.

Just as choosing a college may have been a big decision for you, choosing a major or a career is also a big decision. You may again be feeling confused, scared, and excited—but this chapter will help you begin getting past these feelings. It's time to start working on your career goals. In the next few pages, you'll learn how to develop appropriate career goals and you'll start figuring out the steps to achieve them.

> **"Goals are dreams with deadlines."**
>
> —*Diana Scharf Hunt*

Begin to Consider Your Career Goals

So far in this book, you've done a lot of work to learn more about yourself. So, now that you've done that, what's next? What are your current career goals? Are you hoping to declare a major? Identify a career you like? Decide whether a certain career is really right for you? As you'll see, the most effective goals are ones that are written down. So, let's start now. Even if you are just scribbling down parts of sentences, take a moment to write down some of your career-related goals. *Example:* Explore my interest in working with computers.

Not Every Goal is a Good Goal

Like many things in the world, it's easy to set a goal, but it isn't always easy to set a good goal. If you don't take the time to set up effective, motivating goals, you may find that you procrastinate and delay starting to work on them, that you lose interest in them over time, or that you fail to reach them altogether. But what makes an effective goal? Here are a few guidelines to keep in mind:

Effective Goals are Specific and Measurable

As you set a goal, make sure that you have enough detail. After all, you need to know what you are working towards, and you need to know when you've accomplished it!

For instance, some students reading a book like this start out with the stated goal of finding a job that they'll enjoy going to every day for the rest of their lives. If that sounds like your goal, though, ask yourself: How will you know when you have accomplished it? On the day you retire and look back over your working life, will you be able to say that you were happy *every* day?

Obviously, when you think about it, it would be great to achieve this, but you'd never realistically know if you've accomplished it: it is neither specific nor measurable. So, if this sounds like one of

your goals, how might you revise it so that you'll know when you've reached it? Instead of challenging yourself to find the one perfect job, you might want to think in terms of generating a list of five solid career fields and researching each one in your career center during the coming weeks. Then, once you have accomplished that goal, you might consider setting another that will help you continue on the path to career satisfaction.

Sometimes big goals need to be broken down in this way. It's impossible to accomplish them all at once, and some people get frustrated because of this. To help yourself get started, it's often much easier to set shorter-term goals that help you progress toward your long-term goal. We'll talk more about this later in this chapter. But first, there are some other characteristics of good goals that you should consider.

Goals Should Be Realistic . . . But Challenging

Take the time to evaluate whether your goal is something that you can realistically accomplish. This can be tricky, because you need to set a goal that is challenging enough to keep you motivated yet is also attainable with hard work.

For instance, Jim was a college sophomore who stated that one of his goals was to raise his GPA to 3.5/4.0, so that he could increase his chances of getting into graduate school. After a rough start during his first year in college, his current GPA was 2.4. Was his goal realistic? Using a GPA calculator on the Internet, he determined that taking a full load of classes, he'd need to get straight-A's for nearly the next two years just to get to his desired GPA. While he developed a strategy to improve his academic work in college, he decided that getting to a 3.5 GPA wasn't truly realistic, and that a 3.25 GPA might be a more reasonable goal. At the same time, he decided to increase his efforts to gain good campus experiences to make himself a better candidate for graduate school.

But just as Jim set his goals too high and had to revise them, make sure that you don't set goals that are too easy to achieve. Inventor

Thomas Edison said, "Opportunity is missed by most people; because it is dressed in overalls and looks like work." Your goal shouldn't be too easy to achieve. Push yourself. Expect that if you've come up with a really good goal, you'll need to work hard to achieve it.

Goals Should Be Written Down and Reviewed Periodically

Obviously, goals can still motivate us if they aren't written down—but there's something special about taking the time to put words down on paper. It's harder. It forces you to clarify your thinking. It means that you'll be able to look back at those words later on and that you'll have to hold yourself accountable for your thoughts.

Look back at the career goals that you wrote down earlier in this chapter. You did write them down, didn't you? If not, you won't have a tangible, permanent record of your starting point. So if you haven't already done so, go back and take the time to do so now. Really.

Once you have something written down, you have a starting point. Maybe after reading the last few pages, you will want to go back and revise the goals to make them more specific, more measurable, or maybe you will need to write new, more realistic goals. Remember that because life doesn't always go as planned, it is important to be flexible and make changes to your long-term goals based on changing circumstances, and to modify both your long- and short-term goals as opportunities present themselves. Throughout the remainder of your college and life journeys, new opportunities and challenges will present themselves. Routinely setting goals, reassessing them, and being flexible enables you to make progress regardless of the direction your life takes.

Developing Action Plans

Have you ever seen the movie *What About Bob*, which starred Bill Murray and Richard Dreyfuss? In it, Bill Murray's psychiatrist tries to help him through his problems by encouraging him to take

"baby steps." Especially when faced with a big goal that will take a long time to achieve, it's human nature to procrastinate. Don't let yourself fall into this trap! Use the "Realizing Your Goals: Action Plans" worksheet in this chapter to break your goals into specific, manageable steps—even baby steps.

For instance, a big goal you might have in the coming year is to find an internship so that you can try out your tentative career choice and start gaining some experience. That's a big goal. Do you know everything you'll need to do in order to accomplish it? Probably not. But you should be able to think of some ways to get started. Look at the "Goal Setting Worksheet" on the following pages. Perhaps one personal obstacle to finding an internship is that you don't know what kinds of internships exist. A natural first step might be to visit your career center to find out what assistance is available. The staff members there, in turn, will probably have suggestions for the future steps you'll need to take to accomplish the goal. But you'll never know what they are until you get started with the first step. Make sure you fill in the "By when?" section with a specific date within the next few weeks, so that you start taking action, because each action taken gives you more confidence to reach your goal. Continue this action process by looking at other obstacles, brainstorming resources to overcome them, and setting deadlines to use those resources. The result is that you will be speeding along towards achieving your monthly goals.

Continue Building On Your Success

At the end of 30 days, you will have hopefully achieved your 30-day goal by completing the items on your action plan (i.e., your weekly goals). To continue to achieve your semester goal, develop another 30-day goal and set of action plans. At the end of the semester, start the process over. If you follow a goal-setting plan consistently, being flexible and open to new opportunities and roadblocks, you will be amazed at how much you can achieve.

According to baseball's Yogi Berra: "You've got to be very careful if you don't know where you are going, because you might not get there." While it's not always easy to follow his logic, his wisdom is clear. Goals help us see the path that we'll be following on the road to success. As you are continuing to research possible careers, and as you begin to implement your career choice,

Instructions for Goal Setting Worksheet

effective goal setting will be one of the keys to ensure your success.

Develop a Semester-long Goal and Two Shorter-term Goals

Look back at the career goals you have written. Create a semester-long goal that you can achieve through your work this semester that will take you closer to achieving the career goal you previously wrote. Remember to keep your goal specific, measurable, realistic, and challenging. What are short-term goals that you can achieve this week and within the next 30 days to lead to the achievement of the longer-term semester goal? Write these goals in the appropriate areas.

At the beginning, achieving a large goal can seem overwhelming. To help you remember your ability to achieve, list some accomplishments you have made in the past year (those that relate to this goal as well as other achievements). You may find that it's easier to envision future successes when you take the time to recall your past successes!

Overcoming the Obstacles to Achieving Your Goals

There are two major types of obstacles that may keep you from achieving your goals. The first are **personal obstacles**, tangible items such as a lack of knowledge in a particular area, limited skills, or not enough time. Examples that typically arise for college students thinking about careers and majors include obstacles such as not knowing what careers are open to people with certain majors, not knowing anyone in the field with whom to conduct an informational interview, or a lack of knowledge about their own skills. Write down as many personal obstacles as you can; later on, you will create shorter-term goals and action plans to get past these personal obstacles.

The second type of obstacle is **fear**. There are many, many fears that accompany choosing a major and career, for instance, fear of making a mistake, fear of failure, fear of not meeting family expectations, or a fear of what peers may think. Writing these fears down is the first step to addressing them; once you have acknowledged them, you can assess to what extent each one keeps you from moving forward and achieving your goal.

Identifying Good and Bad Habits

Think about your behaviors and habits. Are there habits that will assist you in achieving this goal (e.g., your ability to prioritize your work, balancing work and enjoyment, rewarding yourself for completing your work, etc.)? Writing these habits down with your goal will remind you to continue to use these habits to reach this goal. Similarly, write down your bad habits (e.g., procrastinating, being easily distracted by friends, putting social rewards ahead of work, etc.). As you feel tempted to fall into these habits, remind yourself how they will keep you from achieving your goal.

Indiana University Career Development Center

Goal Setting Worksheet

Goal

By the end of the semester, I will:

To begin accomplishing this goal, within the next 30 days, I will:

Within the next week, I will:

Achievements

Within the past year:

Obstacles

Personal:

Fears:

Habits

Good habits:

Bad habits:

Using Your Human Resources

The last step in setting your goals is to assess who can help you in achieving your goal. Family members, friends, staff members, and professors at your college, or others may be able to provide assistance as you are working towards your goals. Make sure that you ask for help from these supporters!

Support

People who can help:

REALIZING YOUR GOALS: ACTION PLANS

GOAL—What do you want to achieve by the end of this month?

First Obstacle

What do you need to reach your goal? Look back to your obstacles & habits for clues.

_____

_____

_____

_____

Priority

What are you going to do? Who do you need to contact? What resources do you need? What appointments do you need to make? By when?

_____

_____

_____

_____

Deadline

Write out your dates in ink.

_____

_____

_____

Second Obstacle

What do you need to reach your goal? Look back to your obstacles & habits for clues.

_____

_____

_____

_____

Priority

What are you going to do? Who do you need to contact? What resources do you need? What appointments do you need to make? By when?

_____

_____

_____

_____

Deadline

Write out your dates in ink.

_____

_____

_____

Third Obstacle

What do you need to reach your goal? Look back to your obstacles & habits for clues.

_____

_____

_____

_____

Priority

What are you going to do? Who do you need to contact? What resources do you need? What appointments do you need to make? By when?

_____

_____

_____

_____

Deadline

Write out your dates in ink.

_____

_____

_____

Indiana University Career Development Center

Setting Goals and Moving Forward

Once you have thought about different careers that might be appropriate for you, and you have begun moving past the blocks that are slowing your progress, you need to think purposefully about the next steps to take. In short, you will need to set some goals.

Goal setting is the process by which we create a picture of our "ideal future"—a picture that allows us to be intentional about today's activities and accomplishments. Done effectively, goal setting allows us to identify those specific activities and strategies that move us toward that ideal future.

In developing career-related goals, pay particular attention to identifying short-term goals that will help you to accomplish your long-term goals. In addition, choose goals that will help you to develop the qualities you will need in a professional job. Many employers have reported that they have found new college graduates to be ill-prepared for the work world. They have identified 10 weaknesses in the applicants' job-preparedness:

Perceived Weaknesses of Today's College Graduates

Unrealistic Expectations

. . . About entry-level opportunities, career advancement promotion timelines. Unrealistic view of the workplace and what they, as candidates, have to offer the employer.

Poor Communication Skills

Lack of enthusiasm and energy during interviews. An inability to write and speak clearly and concisely with audience needs in mind. Poor spelling and grammar.

No Practical Work Experience

No relevant "real life" experience such as internships, cooperative education, part-time work or meaningful volunteer work.

Lack of Initiative and Work Ethics

No "Go Get It!" attitude. An unwillingness to work long hours and "do what it takes" to do a job and do it well.

Minimal Knowledge and Understanding of the World of Work

Poor research skills. No demonstrated understanding of the industry, organization, competitors, job market, or position.

Inappropriate Attitudes

Lack of patience and a desire for immediate "paybacks." An unwillingness to be coached and a dissatisfaction with lateral broadening instead of career ladder progression.

Undesirable Personal Qualities

Inflexibility. Lack of loyalty and commitment. Poorly developed ethics. Lack of confidence.

Poorly Developed Interpersonal and Teamwork Skills

No evidence that they can work and contribute as part of a diverse team.

Lack of Career Direction and Goals

Failure to adequately assess personal interests, values, and skills to set goals accordingly. A tendency to choose jobs which do not suit them.

Absence of Critical Transferable Skills

Poorly developed math, analytical, reading, and foreign language skills. An inability to demonstrate time management, creativity, and leadership.

Reference: Lindquist, V.R. (1991). *The Northwestern Lindquist-Endicott report: Trends in the employment of college and university graduates in business and industry.* Evanston, IL: Placement Center, Northwestern University.

But don't despair! Just by reading the book in your hands, you have started to address some of these perceived weaknesses. For instance, you have researched various majors and careers and have assessed whether or not your skills and values fit them. However, you might still need to develop the transferable skills or communication skills that your career will require.

Setting Goals and Moving Forward, continued

As is true of any other tool used during our career development process, the quality of the goals we set will determine their usefulness. According to the **S.M.A.R.T.** System developed by Kenneth Blanchard and Spencer Johnson, the most effective, useful goals meet five key criteria:

Goals should be *Specific.* Use the activities from previous chapters to make your goals as clear and focused as possible.

> Needs Work: I want to work with people.

> Much Better: I want to plan social and educational programs for children and adolescents.

Goals should be *Measurable.* You will be unable to determine whether or not you are achieving your goals, if you have no yardstick for measuring outcomes.

> Needs Work: I want to do well in my classes.

> Much Better: I want to earn a 3.0 cumulative GPA this year.

Goals should be *Attainable.* Setting unattainable goals will set you up for failure. Strike a balance by drafting realistic goals that challenge you.

> Needs Work: I want to earn my Ph.D. within one year of graduation.

> Much Better: I want to earn my Ph.D. within five years of finishing my B.A.

Goals should be *Relevant.* Is this goal consistent with other goals you have established? Does it really fit with your immediate and long-range plans?

> Needs Work: I wish to thoroughly review each career listed in the *Occupational Outlook Handbook.*

> Much Better: I will read the seven sections on communications and visual arts occupations in the *Occupational Outlook Handbook.*

Goals should be *Trackable.* How will you know whether or not you're actually moving toward your goal? Establishing trackable goals will allow you to monitor your progress.

> Needs Work: I want improve my public speaking.

> Much Better: I will make two public speeches each month and have faculty and friends evaluate my performance.

Applying these criteria to your own goal setting allows you to move steadily toward your longer range goals, while helping you identify those strategies and tactics that fail to move you forward. Take time now to practice using S.M.A.R.T. techniques as you establish your own goals.

Mapping Out the World of Work

Understanding What's Out There

By Sloane Boyd, Lorenda Schrader, Karen Bazur, and Sue Sgambelluri

IN THIS CHAPTER YOU WILL:

➤ Gain an understanding of what it takes to succeed in today's workplace

➤ Grasp the value of difference—and its potential for enhancing organizational success

➤ Consider the impact of technology on our lives and work

➤ Learn how world markets and their impact on the global economy will influence your work choices

CHAPTER 9
Roadmap of the Working World

The work world is always changing and evolving. As you work in a variety of organizations, you will come to realize—if you haven't already—that work environments and expectations of employees today are in many cases different from those of your grandparents—and maybe even those of your parents. Some of these differences include recent workplace trends such as:

- fewer levels of management

- less promise of lifetime employment with the same employer

- expectations that employees need to continually learn new skills

- employees have more freedom AND responsibility for making decisions regarding their day-to-day work and for charting their own career paths

- increased team approach

- diversified work-force

As employees chart their careers, they also have new options to consider. These options include regular, full-time positions as well as contract or temporary positions. People in contract positions often feel like a "free agent," and these positions often pay a high hourly rate. They often, however, don't include benefits such as retirement, health insurance, or paid vacation days. Some companies hire entry-level people as contract workers to see how well they perform, and after this trial period, they may be hired as regular, full-time employees.

In general, companies hire and retain people as core employees when their work performance demonstrates commitment to and directly benefits the customers. To demonstrate your commitment to an employer and its customers, follow the Rules for Workplace Success discussed in the next section.

Rules for Workplace Success

To succeed at work—whether you're working in a part-time job or internship during school or the summer, or in a full-time job after graduation—there are some tried and true basic rules for success, and some advanced rules for long-term success, especially in the current work world.

Understanding Employers' Expectations

> "The new vocation is not in the field of electronics, genetic engineering or international trade. The new vocation exists within every field, for it requires not that one produce some particular new thing, but rather that one develop a new way of being productive."
>
> —*William Bridges*

The Basics

These rules are basic and may seem obvious—but they are so important, you want to be sure you know these inside and out, and that you follow them as often as you possibly can, in every work setting.

Arrive on time—or even a few minutes early. This will build a strong and lasting positive impression. This becomes especially important when you make your first mistake—which will happen, because it happens to everyone. See the box below for more about what happens when you make a mistake—especially a big one.

Pay attention to details, be as accurate as you can, and learn from your mistakes. It's often the details that make the difference between doing a really good job and doing just a satisfactory job. Strive to be excellent in everything you do.

Meet deadlines and communicate along the way. Keep your supervisor and your co-workers informed of your progress. If it looks like you're not going to make a deadline, let others know as soon as you realize this. Then your supervisor can either set a new deadline or re-distribute work as needed to ensure an essential deadline is met.

Demonstrate that you can work without supervision. When you encounter an obstacle, think of a solution—or two or three—then propose these to your supervisor and co-workers.

Seek guidance when you need it. Ask if you don't understand or are unsure. Then listen carefully to the responses you receive, and act accordingly. Asking questions shows you want to do the best job possible.

Accept change willingly and work hard at learning new things. Seek opportunities to grow. If you have time, offer to help your supervisor or a co-worker with a project that wasn't assigned to you. (Again, remember first get your work done on time, and keep your supervisor informed about what you're doing.)

Treat everyone with respect, regardless of their status within the organization.

—BASICS are adapted from The Career Adventure, Johnston, Susan M. (Chap. 11)

Advanced Rules

As you master the basic rules, stretch yourself a bit and try out the advanced rules for success.

- Don't let yourself get too comfortable—always keep learning and make yourself multi-skilled and flexible.

What happens when you make a mistake at work?

When you make a mistake, your supervisor is likely to conclude one of two things, depending on the impression she or he has of you and your work. If you consistently behave in ways that follow the rules for success, then your supervisor will think you are a conscientious, bright, hard-working person who does your best, and just like all of us, you just made a mistake. If you have followed the rules for success, they'll think this even when it's a huge mistake—one that costs the organization thousands of dollars! If you have not taken the rules for success seriously and "slacked off," thinking to yourself this is just a part-time job that's not very important or glamorous, then your supervisor will credit your mistake to your abilities—or inabilities—and to a poor attitude. Your supervisor will likely think or say, "S/he doesn't really care, and s/he has not really done a very good job since the day s/he started." First impressions do count—and when you're in a new job—no matter whether it's part-time or full-time—you're creating a first impression every day for the first few months or even the first year. Until you make your first big mistake, then the impression you've made will become clear—and it will stick for a long time.

- Attend and participate in professional conferences. This will allow you to keep up with trends in your profession and to continue making new contacts.

- Seek new projects that will help you learn new skills.

- Take classes and seek certifications to build your knowledge base.

- Find ways to contribute to the success of your organization. Think of yourself as a partner with your employer in learning how to do business better and how to respond to changes in the economy.

- Go a step beyond taking on new responsibilities and proposing solutions—initiate new ideas and projects. You may need to be careful about when and how you do this. Consult with someone more experienced than you, someone you respect, such as a mentor in your organization or from a previous job or a professor in one of your classes.

- Learn all you can about your work culture. What are the specific "rules for success" in your organization? These are known as "workplace politics." Again, find a mentor or two, and ask them how things get done and who has formal and informal power and authority in your organization.

- Learn your organization's technological capabilities and keep up with changes.

- Network! Get to know people in other divisions of your organization or in related industries. Volunteer for team projects; participate in company-wide meetings or social events; be open and friendly. You never know when you might need to use a connection to get a new job or develop a new resource.

- Keep up with the news. Local, national and international politics, scientific discoveries, and economic trends influence organizational decisions every day.

Adaptability in the Workplace

As part of your college experience, you have probably experienced diversity. Perhaps it was interaction with an international student, a physically-challenged student, someone from a different region of this country, someone of a different ethnic background, or different socio-economic background, or different religion, sexual orientation, or even someone older than you (professors count too!). The fact is, this country specializes in allowing for differences—our culture is designed to allow, and sometimes encourage, diversity. A university campus is a microcosm of the world, and it may be your first real opportunity to interact with other cultures. Make the most of your college experience: try other things, explore actively, visit cultural centers, attend cultural events, expose yourself to as much as you can. There are safety nets in place—forums where your interactions are part of a group, discussions where you can examine your emotions, opportunities to disengage from an uncomfortable situation.

As you enter the work force, most of these safety nets go away. You may sit next to someone who speaks to their spouse in another language, or you may serve on a committee that includes a deaf person who requires an interpreter, or you may work in an industry where the factory personnel deal with a whole set of socio-economic factors that you've never experienced (long-standing cash-flow problems, single-parenthood, drugs, physical response to disagreements, etc.). You can't walk away, and you can't avoid interactions. What you can do is develop an open mind, find new ways to cope, and try to understand that there are many ways to accomplish goals. This is not a new concept. We discussed the concept of "mutual usefulness," when you studied your MBTI results in Chapter 4.

Embracing Diversity

The first step to embracing diversity, is to understand that diversity works. Different viewpoints allow businesses to anticipate market reactions and to develop universally accepted policies and products. An understanding of foreign cultures leads to more influence in world markets. A colleague who is different from you can think outside of your box, and may arrive at creative solutions that you miss.

The second step in accepting diversity is to realize that you, personally, have cultural filters in place—no matter how open you try

The Value of Diversity

"There never was in the world two opinions alike, no more than two hairs or two grains; the most universal quality is diversity."

—*Montaigne (1533-1592)*

"It's not what you say, it's what you do. If you're not part of the future, then get out of the way."

—*John Mellencamp, Peaceful World*

to be, you, like the rest of us, are programmed to think and act within your own concepts of right and wrong. There's nothing wrong with that, as long as we realize that our filters need to be cleaned occasionally, and that filters that others use are being applied to your words, actions, and attitudes as well. Be aware when you are judging someone, and ask yourself if their actions are "wrong" in all cultures, or just in yours. Try to concentrate on results, more than methods.

The third step in appreciating diversity is to make it a personal challenge to understand people and cultures that are different from your own. Remember the old Native American saying, "Walk a mile in my moccasins?" That's a good principle to apply. Don't be afraid to ask someone, in a non-confron-tational moment, to talk about his or her culture. Most will be thrilled that you are interested, and you'll find that understanding will lead to much more effective communication in the future.

The chances that you will not find diversity in your work place are very slim. In 1999, the Bureau of Labor Statistics projected that, by 2008, there will be six million more jobs available than there will be people to fill them. The demographic shift due to our aging population will almost certainly ensure that these jobs will be filled by people who have grown up in different cultures. Successful employers will be those who have the most open, flexible, and creative hiring policies. Successful employees will be those with the best multicultural skills.

Food for Thought
If the world were a village of 1,000 people

- 584 would be Asians
- 123 would be Africans
- 95 would be East and West Europeans
- 84 would be Latin Americans
- 55 Soviets and former Soviets
- 52 North Americans
- 6 Australians and New Zealanders
- 165 people would speak Mandarin
- 86 would speak English
- 83 Hindi/Urdu
- 64 Spanish
- 58 Russian
- 37 Arabic
- 500 would speak Bengali, Portuguese, Indonesian, Japanese, German, French, and 200 other languages

- 300 Christians
- 175 Muslims
- 128 Hindus
- 55 Buddhists
- 47 Animists
- 210 all other religions, including atheists
- 330 would be children
- 60 would be over the age of 65
- 200 people would receive three-fourths of the income
- 200 would receive only two percent of the income
- 70 would own an automobile (some more than one)
- 670 adults would be illiterate

—Adapted from "State of the Village Report," by Donella Meadows, in The Global Citizen, 1990.

It's a Different World

We hear the word "technology" and think that if we're not computer science students, the rest of the sentence doesn't apply to us. But take one day and walk around the town in which you live. Look for instances of technology at work: some grocery stores use computers in the produce department so that customers can weigh and price their own produce—some even have a check out that is totally automated. Simply scan your items, scan your credit card, bag your items, and you're out. You'll see evidence of technological changes in almost every organization.

Governments are automating their processes. "E-Gov" is a concept that is being embraced by not only the federal government, but by state and local governments as well. In many places you can get all the forms you need for any governmental service online. You can purchase hunting licenses online, pay parking tickets online, and pay your taxes online. And e-government is still in its infancy.

So no matter what your major is, you will be affected by technology. And change, indeed, is in the air. The healthcare field is wide open with positions ranging from nursing (because of the aging baby boomers) to the pharmaceutical field. The biotech industry is on the rise with genome research and other biological developments. And these fields are not only looking for science backgrounds; remember that each of these organizations needs professionals in human resources, public relations, finance and budgeting, and management.

How Technology has Changed the Way We Look at Jobs

"Technology is dominated by two types of people: those who understand what they do not manage, and those who manage what they do not understand."

—*Putt's Law*

"Chance favors the prepared mind."

—*Quoted in H. Eves Return to Mathematical Circles, Prindle, Wever and Schmidt, Boston, 1988.*

How to Be Prepared

While in college it's important to get exposure to as much technology as possible. Most of us use e-mail and word processing. Try to learn and use as many applications as you can; for example, look for opportunities to learn how to use spreadsheets. If you have to give presentations in class, try to learn how to use presentation software, such as PowerPoint. Get on the Internet and do research online for your papers. You might even want to build a personal Web page or put your resume online.

You'll become valuable to employers by entering the job market with some technology skills, and you don't have to be a programmer to know these things. More importantly, you show that you understand that the world is changing, and it's changing quickly. You show that you are open to change and can adapt.

Exercises to Try

As we become more aware of changes in technology, examples of those things seem to appear everywhere.

Over a period of a few days, carry a notebook with you and make note of technology in the workplace. You might see examples at the grocery store, the mall, you might see cameras and signs at stoplights that are automatically clocking the speed of every car that passes. Try to find 10 examples.

Look for places in your community or school where you can take classes or learn how to use certain technologies. For example, does your school offer extra classes or workshops in how to use presentation software, databases, or spreadsheets? Write down the resources you have available to you in learning how to get additional skills.

Go Global!

With global communication networks and with technology that links *entire continents* as easily as it links companies, you truly will live and work in a global environment. Even if your career never takes you overseas, you will, in all likelihood, work for an organization that is affected by global economic trends and relies on the global marketplace in some way.

So what can you do—now—to begin preparing for opportunities in this environment?

- **Build the Basics**—Regardless of where your career leads, your value to an organization will always depend on your ability to problem-solve, to work as part of a team, and to demonstrate initiative, flexibility, resourcefulness, and sound decision-making. From your earliest days on campus, seek out opportunities that sharpen these *basic, transferable skills (see Page 24)*. A career consultant or advisor can help you identify student organizations, part-time jobs, internships, and volunteer experiences that will enhance these abilities.

Planning and Preparing for the Global Job Market

"A man's feet should be planted in his country, but his eyes should survey the world."

—*George Santayana (1863-1952)*

Researching Global Companies

U.S. Chamber of Commerce

World Trade Center

Int'l. Trade Division in each state

Country Web Sites

Major Foreign Newspapers

International Agencies

Directories in your campus career center

Embassy Web sites

World Chamber of Commerce

United Nations and UNDP Agencies

Peace Corps

International Search Engines—for example, www.GlobalConnector.org

Don't overlook the U.S. Government as an international employer!

language (even if your major doesn't require it!). Attend cultural events on campus. Participate in your school's study abroad program. If at all possible, travel overseas as your resources allow. The greater your comfort level with a wide variety of individuals and settings, the more confident you can be in pursuing a position that depends on the global work environment.

- **Begin Locally**—Interested in a career in human services in a developing nation? Look to your local United Way or Red Cross chapters and research possible internships with these international organizations. Eager to work in China or Japan? Consider interning with organizations headquartered in Seattle, San Francisco, Los Angeles, or other cities that serve as a domestic "springboard" to overseas trade with those countries. Research multi-national companies where you may have a choice of working in an overseas branch. In other words, begin planning and preparing for an international career before you ever travel overseas. Begin by using resources in your own backyard.

- **Build "Cross-Cultural Competence"**—Pursue activities and experiences that allow you to interact with the widest variety of people possible. Become fluent, or at least proficient, in a foreign

Follow these basic strategies—and remember the tremendous resource you have in your campus career center—and you truly *will* find "a *world* of opportunities" in your career. Good luck!

ADDITIONAL RESOURCES

Exercise

FORCED CHOICE VALUES CONFLICTS

OBJECTIVE:

To illustrate the need to prioritize one's values and separate the "need to haves" from the merely "nice to haves".

THE ACTIVITY:

Use the following dilemmas to stimulate in-class group discussion or as the basis for individual student writing projects. Invite students to discuss the rationale for their responses and the value system they use to make their decisions.

1. Family Consideration vs. Achievement and Upward Mobility

You work in an up-and-coming marketing firm. You are being considered for a promotion. An important account is racing against a deadline, and your boss has asked you to work overtime. However, it is your daughter's birthday, and you promised to be home to celebrate her birthday with her. Which do you choose?

2. Pay and Routine Work vs. Variety

You have been offered two jobs. One job pays extremely well ($40,000) but the work is very routine and structured. The other job pays very little ($15,000) but has a lot of variety (e.g., some leadership, some working with people, some research and writing, some data analysis, etc.) Which job do you choose?

3. Pay, Achievement, and Prestige vs. Moral Values

You work for a chemical company and have just been appointed vice president of production. You receive a $100,000 salary and are highly regarded among people in your company and your community. You learn that, through no fault of your own, employees of your company have been illegally dumping chemical wastes. You realize that if you turn this information over to the authorities, you may lose your job and the company may go broke. What do you do?

4. Location and Controlled Environment vs. Self-Expression and Creativity

You have been offered two jobs. One is in a perfect geographic location (e.g. near mountains or an ocean) and allows you to pursue your leisure interests, but the working environment is fairly controlled. There are many rules and you receive constant supervision. The second job is in a less ideal location, but it offers you a lot of opportunities for self-expression and creativity. Which do you choose?

5. Variety and Leadership vs. Autonomy or Independence

You already work in a job where you exercise considerable leadership over others. In addition, the job offers a wide variety of activities and you are never bored. However, you have an opportunity to join your best friend in starting your own business. Which do you choose?

JOURNAL ENTRY TOPICS FOR PROCESSING IDENTIFIED INTERESTS

Note: The following topics can be used after the Interests lesson or discussion. If a student has taken the Strong Interest Inventory (and has had an interpretation by a qualified counselor) or another interest inventory/exercise, the following topics can be used as reflection topics:

➤ Using your interest inventory results and your own judgment, identify your Holland Theme Code (RIASEC). Refer back to your textbook and supplemental resources for detailed descriptions; write about those specific personal qualities and interests that most accurately describe you. As you research career or majors, look carefully for fields that require individuals with these qualities and interests.

➤ Write about three examples of activities you have done in the past that "fit" with your interest theme code. Identify some specific activities that will allow you to continue exploring your interests.

➤ The list of 10 occupations on your Strong Interest Inventory Occupational Scales represents a starting point for your research. Use the resources in the career section of your campus library to gather information about these occupations. Begin learning about the types of individuals that tend to be most successful, and then evaluate the degree to which each career option matches your interests.

➤ Describe a work setting and/or occupation that would provide you with the opportunity to explore or maintain each of your interests.

Exercise

A PERSONALITY PREFERENCE EXERCISE

Note: The following exercise can be used by instructors/counselors to assist students in processing their personality preferences. If students have taken the Myers-Briggs Type Indicator, they must also have had an interpretation by a qualified counselor in order to complete the following exercise. The exercise can also be used by an individual who has taken an informal version of the MBTI® personality preferences. Students are also encouraged to use supplemental resources to enhance their understanding of their preferences. Refer to the suggested reading list in chapter 4 of this book.

Write a paper using the following guidelines:

➤ List your reported MBTI® type.

➤ Are your MBTI results an accurate portrayal of your personality preferences?

➤ If you agree with the reported type, give *three or four specific examples* from your everyday life that demonstrate the reported type is a good fit. For example, if the MBTI indicates that you have a preference for "I" (Introversion), *describe (do not list)* a situation during which you clearly showed your preference. Give specific examples.

➤ If you disagree with any of your preferences, list each one and explain why it is not an accurate representation of your preferences in life. Additionally, if you feel that a different type code reflects your preferences more precisely, list that code and give *specific example situations* to justify your analysis.

➤ Identify strengths and weaknesses that you associate with your type.

➤ Look at some of the careers you are considering; will these career options allow you to work in a setting that enhances your strengths? Explain.

➤ What other career options would allow you to foster these strengths?

Exercise

JOURNAL ENTRY TOPICS FOR PROCESSING IDENTIFIED SKILLS

Note: The following topics can be used after students have identified their skills in chapter 2 of this book. Topics can be written on the board as "food for thought" or journal entries after a lesson or discussion.

➤ As you think about the future, describe a setting in which you will use the skills you enjoy best every day. Describe your ideal setting focusing on skills used in that job.

➤ Name three careers that you are considering. Which of these options best fits your list of preferred skills?

➤ What other careers may match your preferred skills?

➤ What skills will you need to develop to reach your career goal?

➤ Identify skills that you think you will always want to use and skills that you strongly prefer not to use in a work setting?

THE CONNECTIONS PROJECT
(An in-class group project adapted from "Making the Connections")

Instructions: Divide the class into groups of no larger than 4-5 students. Hand each group the title and brief description of an occupation (a sample list has been provided on page 137). Each group is to look up the detailed description of that occupation and assign values, skills, a Holland Theme Code, and an MBTI® type to the occupation based on the description. As they discuss the duties, they are to justify their reasons for ascribing the values, skills, Holland Theme Code, and the MBTI® type.

Title of Occupation: _____

Values (Use your values list from Chapter 1):

_____ _____ _____

_____ _____ _____

List reasons these values match the occupation:

_____

_____

_____

Skills (Use the Skills list from the skills chapter in this book or the Skillscan Profile):

_____ _____ _____

_____ _____ _____

Justify skills needed for this occupation:

_____

_____

_____

Holland Theme Code: _____   _____   _____
(Strong Interest Inventory)

(RIASEC)   **Reasons:**

_____   _____

_____   _____

_____   _____

MBTI:

_____   _____   _____   _____

(Personality Preferences)   E or I   S or N   T or F   J or P

Reasons:

E or I _____   _____

_____

S or N _____   _____

_____

T or F _____   _____

_____

J or P _____   _____

_____

Sample Occupational Titles
to use with THE CONNECTIONS PROJECT

Below is a list of sample occupational titles to use with "The Connections Project" exercise. They are not complete descriptions. Students can either use the books in their career library to find full descriptions or use online resources suggested by a career counselor or instructor.

The following source is helpful and has concise descriptions of career titles:

Occupational Outlook Handbook (2002). Electronic Version: http://stats.bls.gov/oco/ocoiab.htm.

Sample Career Titles & Brief Descriptions

Teachers

"Teachers act as facilitators or coaches, using interactive discussions and "hands-on" learning to help students learn and apply concepts in subjects such as science, mathematics, or English . . . ."

Source: Occupational Outlook Handbook. [Electronic Version]. http://stats.bls.gov/oco/ocoiab.htm.

Psychologists

"Psychologists study the human mind and human behavior. Research psychologists investigate . . . ."

Source: Occupational Outlook Handbook. [Electronic Version]. http://stats.bls.gov/oco/ocoiab.htm.

Lawyers

"Lawyers, also called attorneys, act both as advocates and advisors in our society. As advocates, they represent one of . . . ."

Source: Occupational Outlook Handbook. [Electronic Version]. http://stats.bls.gov/oco/ocoiab.htm.

Retail Salesperson

"Whether selling shoes, computer equipment, or automobiles, retail salespersons assist customers in finding what they are looking for and try to interest them in buying . . . ."

Source: Occupational Outlook Handbook. [Electronic Version]. http://stats.bls.gov/oco/ocoiab.htm.

Announcers

"Announcers in radio and television perform a variety of tasks on and off the air. They announce station program information . . . ."

Source: Occupational Outlook Handbook. [Electronic Version]. http://stats.bls.gov/oco/ocoiab.htm.

Registered Nurse

"Registered nurses (R.N.s) work to promote health, prevent disease, and help patients cope with illness. They are advocates and health educators for patients, families . . . ."

Source: Occupational Outlook Handbook. [Electronic Version]. http://stats.bls.gov/oco/ocoiab.htm.

Correctional Officer

"Correctional officers are responsible for overseeing individuals who have been arrested and are awaiting trial or who have been convicted of a crime and sentenced to serve time in a jail, reformatory, or penitentiary. They maintain security . . . ."

Source: Occupational Outlook Handbook. [Electronic Version]. http://stats.bls.gov/oco/ocoiab.htm.

Rehabilitation Counselors

"Rehabilitation counselors help people deal with the personal, social, and vocational effects of disabilities. They counsel people with disabilities resulting from birth defects, illness or disease, accidents, or the stress of daily life. . . ."

Source: Occupational Outlook Handbook. [Electronic Version]. http://stats.bls.gov/oco/ocoiab.htm.

Biological and Medical Scientists

"Biological and medical scientists study living organisms and their relationship to their environment. They research problems. . . ."

Source: Occupational Outlook Handbook. [Electronic Version]. http://stats.bls.gov/oco/ocoiab.htm.

Perceived Weaknesses of Today's College Graduates

Unrealistic Expectations

. . . about entry level opportunities, career advancement and promotion timelines. Unrealistic view of the workplace and what they, as candidates, have to offer the employer.

No Practical Work Experience

No relevant "real life" experience such as internships, cooperative education, part-time work or meaningful volunteer work.

Minimal Knowledge and Understanding of the World of Work

Poor research skills. No demonstrated understanding of the industry, organization, competitors, job market, or position.

Undesirable Personal Qualities

Inflexibility. Lack of loyalty and commitment. Poorly developed ethics. Lack of confidence.

Lack of Career Direction and Goals

Failure to adequately assess personal interests, values, and skills and to set goals accordingly. A tendency to choose jobs which do not suit them.

Poor Communication Skills

Lack of enthusiasm and energy during interviews. An inability to write and speak clearly and concisely with audience needs in mind. Poor spelling and grammar.

Lack of Initiative and Work Ethic

No "Go Get It" attitude. An unwillingness to work long hours and "do what it takes" to do a job and do it well.

Inappropriate Attitudes

Lack of patience and a desire for immediate "paybacks." An unwillingness to be coached and a dissatisfaction with lateral broadening instead of career ladder progression.

Poorly Developed Interpersonal and Teamwork Skills

No evidence that they can work and contribute as part of a diverse team.

Absence of Critical Transferable Skills

Poorly developed math, analytical, reading and foreign language skills. An inability to demon- strate time management, creativity, and leadership.

Reference: Lindquist, V.R. (1991). *The Northwestern Lindquist-Endicott report: Trends in the employment of college and university graduates in business and industry.* Evanston, IL: Placement Center, Northwestern University.

About the Authors

Sloane Boyd

Career Development Center/Arts and Sciences Placement Office—Indiana University

Growing up I loved to learn, and I didn't think much about what I would do for a career. During college, I discovered there were hundreds of career options. What helped me explore these options most was talking with people, volunteering, and doing two internships. I loved my internship as a Peer Counselor in the career center, though it took me a few years before I realized I wanted to focus my career in this field. In 16 years, I've worked in a variety of positions, in fields as diverse as financial consulting, interior decorating, technology management, and career development. The qualities that have helped me be successful in these different settings are: giving my all and doing the best I can; taking initiative and offering solutions to problems; and constantly learning and stretching myself (even when it feels really uncomfortable). As a manager, I also look for these traits in staff members on my team, so we can provide the highest quality services and products and continually improve ways of "doing business"—whatever our "business" is. Having experiences in different settings, and recognizing the value of the qualities above, gives me confidence when seeking promotions or making career changes, either because my own dreams and desires change, or because circumstances and the world around me change. In my current position as Interim Director of our center, I find myself experiencing some of the greatest changes and challenges in my career so far. I'm learning and stretching nearly every day . . . and I love it; I wouldn't want it any other way.

Jennifer DeSana

Career Development Center/Arts and Sciences Placement Office—Indiana University

There is one very memorable book that had an impression on my career path as a young child, *Girls Can be Anything,* by Norma Klein. This book inspired me to become anything I wanted to be. I had dreams of becoming the *first* female President, an Olympic athlete, a teacher, a lawyer, and a doctor. Eventually, when I entered college, I had to make choices about my career, and ultimately I decided that helping people was the most rewarding and noble career I could choose. This value, as well as my work experience, influenced me to teach special education, become a career counselor, and an academic advisor. I still have visions of pursuing careers in a variety of fields and know that my career path will continue to evolve and change, but my dedication to helping people will always be a component of any job I choose.

Arlene Hill

Career Development Center/Arts and Sciences Placement Office—Indiana University

Although I dreamed of being a singer/actor when I sang my first solo at the age of 5, I knew that I valued stability, and turned toward more "practical" careers. Throughout high school, I continued to act and sing, but refused to major in theater in college; instead of trying to find a balance between my love of performing and need for stability, I denied my passion and drifted through five majors. Finally, I fully analyzed my values and realized I was only truly happy when I was performing. I set a goal to perform full time and created action plans to identify theaters and prepare for auditions, which led to a full time summer theater job. I loved the experience and decided to pursue performing professionally. So, for six years in Chicago, I was a professional singer/actor, with a "practical day-job" in financial services. When an illness stopped me from performing, I received career counseling (including the MBTI and Strong) and realized that my own experiences could be used to help others understand and pursue their vocational passions.

Sally Gerrish

Georgia Institute of Technology/Emory Center for the Engineering of Living Tissues

It seems from high school on, I always wanted and sought to be a counselor. Once in college, I knew it was counseling in the school system that peaked my interest the most. Not until graduate school did I become introduced to career counseling and working with undergraduate students to spur thoughts, help them find direction, and listen to their ideas. What is my passion? What is it that makes me truly enjoy coming to work everyday? It is having a real desire to help students as they search for career choices. Working at Indiana University in the Career Development Center and now at Georgia Institute of Technology, though very different jobs, the students have the same questions, same desires to find a satisfying career paths, and I enjoy helping them make that happen.

Allison Keller

Career Center—University of Notre Dame

I began my undergraduate years at Stanford University with little idea of what I wanted to do following graduation. Due to my broad interests, I decided to take a variety of courses and eventually chose Psychology as my major. In addition to academics, I became very involved in the peer academic advising program and the peer counseling program at our Career Center. My experiences outside of the classroom were probably the most influential in deciding what I wanted to do after graduation. After completing my degree, I decided to continue my education and pursue my passion of working with and advising students. I directly entered the Master's program in Higher Education and Student Affairs at Indiana University. During graduate school, I served two years as a graduate assistant at the Career Development Center. This experience reinforced my interest in student affairs, and more specifically career counseling. I am currently a Career Counselor at the University of Notre Dame. I greatly enjoy the college campus environment, interaction with students, and program planning and development. In the future, I hope to continue learning, re-assessing my career decisions, and pursuing my passions.

Olivia Martinez

Career Development Center/Arts and Sciences Placement Office—Indiana University

For as long as I can remember, I have had a strong desire for self-expression and helping others. I was performing mariachi music in front of my family and family friends at the age of two; I started baby-sitting and tutoring at the age of nine; I was the family counselor at the age of 13. My experiences teaching at Adam's Hill Elementary in San Antonio and advising students at Stanford University's Undergraduate Advising Center allowed me to experience the joys of working with a team of professionals who were passionately committed to students' success. Having the encouragement and mentoring from Stanford professor and prominent career theorist, John Krumboltz, provided me with the motivation I needed to pursue the field of career counseling. My career path has taken me on some wonderful adventures and challenges. Working at Indiana University has allowed me to combine my strongest passions of self-expression and helping others in a creative and independent way. It allows me the independence I need, and the variety and excitement I require, along with the value of helping students in a professional and rewarding environment. I love what I do. I hope this book will help you to find your passions and pursue them with vigor!

Daniel Pascoe

Career Development Center/Arts and Sciences Placement Office—Indiana University

I was born and raised in Mexico, a country where I rarely heard about career development in academic environments. I was expected to pursue one career from young adulthood to potential retirement. I remember having decided early in my life that I would study at a University to become a designer. Well, towards the end of my degree in Industrial Design, I learned that my heart was where people were and my vocation where people could be. Thus, I left my country and moved to the United States to attend Divinity School. After ministering among youth and congregations in Mexico and the U.S. for over a decade, I decided to explore the field of social services and soon became the director of a crisis center for homeless families. I enjoyed helping others, but still knew there was a better match for me. Five years later, I moved to Indiana University to assume my current placement in the Career Development Center and begin Ph.D. studies in Education. I have realized that the secret to healthy career development is continuous exploration. Today, I truly enjoy working in the career development field, one that allows me to counsel, teach, and administer programs for the vocational exploration and career growth of many college students.

Jeremy Podany

Career Development Center/Arts and Sciences Placement Office—Indiana University

I find it rather encouraging that the three most desired career areas of people with my Myers-Briggs personality profile are Arts, Teaching, and Religion, because those summarize my life roles thus far. In my teens, I loved being on stage; I would always sing at home, create videos in place of tests for a class grade, and enroll myself in speech and theatre classes. In college, although I changed my major three times, it was all within the area of Secondary Education. Teaching continued for me after college, but not in the classroom, as I worked part-time in university residence halls and part-time with a collegiate ministry. As I reflect on the past and on my personality profile, I understand why I am so satisfied in my current role of teaching a career development class and counseling university students.

Elena Polenova

Career Center—Stony Brook University (SUNY)

I grew up in a country where career decisions were to be made by the age of 17 and never changed. I decided to become a psychologist because I was always interested in other people's problems, sensitive, and prone to endless self-reflection. The first 10 years of my professional life were spent as a crisis counselor. When I moved to the United States, I was fascinated by the mobility of the society but slightly overwhelmed by all the choices people have. I threw

myself into career exploration including theater, international business, real estate, and cross-cultural research. The need to settle down brought me to the Career Center at Stony Brook for advice. I walked out of there totally loving what they do and wanting to be one of them. I eventually joined this wonderful office and am still very happy here. I am a curious person by nature, who enjoys meeting new people and traveling, loves change, and welcomes the unknown. My current job is a great match to my personality at this stage of its development.

Lorenda Schrader

Career Development Center/International Services—Indiana University

I grew up in a mid-sized, homogenous, Midwestern town, and was never "different." I was fascinated by anything international, however, and, after completing degrees in Political Science and French, relocated to Washington, D.C. There, for the first time, I experienced real diversity. I was a minority in my own nation's capitol! I was taught, sometimes gently, and sometimes forcibly, how to understand and work with others. Since then, I have traveled, worked, and studied abroad in Europe and Africa, and have worked with people from around the world. Now, I interact with people of different cultures all the time, and learn more about them—and myself—on a daily basis. It's truly a small world.

Marianna Savoca

Career Center—Stony Brook University (SUNY)

I was to become a professional athlete; at least that's what I thought at age 12. My dreams changed often—gymnast, Olympic swimmer, and a centerfielder for the New York Mets. After excelling in math and science in high school, I considered becoming an orthopedic surgeon. In college at SUNY Binghamton, two things happened—I lost interest in science and found a work-study job as a student assistant in the Career Development Center. I loved my job. I loved helping students. I became the unofficial resume reviewer on my floor and CDC spokesperson in my dorm. Years later, I now direct a staff of people just like me—people who love helping students find their passions and helping them make it happen. It's a very rewarding career that I suspect I will enjoy for a long time to come.

Sue Sgambelluri

Career Development Center/Arts and Sciences Placement Office—Indiana University

From a physical therapist (at age 8) to a politician (at age 12) to a theater manager (at age 17) to a retail manager (at age 20), I clearly went through a range of career ideas before I truly found my niche. Just by watching people around me, I came to realize that connecting people with careers they love (careers in which they would spend a lot of their time each day) is Important Work (capitalized on purpose!) Once I realized how much I enjoyed this work, I then needed to choose a work setting that I would enjoy . . . and I couldn't think of any environment that would be more fun than a university. Now I have the best of several worlds . . . I do the kind of work I enjoy (and I train others how to do it!) in a setting I love—Indiana University.

Paul Timmins

Career and Community Learning Center— University of Minnesota

Growing up, I never had a clear idea of what career I wanted to pursue, but was fortunate to be surrounded by people who encouraged me to try things out so I could discover what I enjoyed doing and set goals for the future. Through various experiences, I learned that I enjoyed giving presentations in public, working with groups of people to solve problems, and helping people individually—and that I really enjoyed doing all of them in the same day. As a college student, I was president of our campus student government and discovered that I enjoyed working on a college campus. Since then, I've received a Master's degree in education and worked in a few different jobs at colleges. I now manage the career services offered in the College of Liberal Arts at the University of Minnesota. I find my work to be rewarding and truly appreciate the variety: in a typical day, I teach career exploration classes, work with colleagues to organize programs for liberal arts students, and help individuals clarify and implement their career goals.

Jan Van Dyke

Career Development Center/Arts and Sciences Placement Office—Indiana University

From being a director of a non-profit organization, a campaign manager for a U.S. congressional candidate, a VISTA volunteer, and a director of career services, I have had a wide variety of jobs. However, they all contain elements of the same career themes: helping others, trying to effect change, organizing resources, and empowering others with information and new insights. These themes match the results of my assessments, which include interests, skills, values, and personality type. My career path illustrates the importance of being open to a variety of career fields and job titles when researching career possibilities. It is also very important not to just read about the different career fields, but to try them out through internships, job shadowing, volunteering and information interviews. I hope that the resources found in Chapter 6 will help you find career fields that match your unique interests, skills, values, and personality type.

Karen Weist

Career Development Center/Arts and Sciences Placement Office—Indiana University

I don't think I could have predicted my career path when I was a child. My childhood dreams included becoming a flight attendant, actress, or mother. I went off to college because my parents expected me to follow my siblings, not because I was pursuing any particular career path. I started out in art, then interior design, education, and finally chose psychology, because I could graduate with that major in the shortest amount of time. Still having no career direction, I spent five years working at various professional jobs, including flight attendant. It was not until I did some volunteer work counseling women with crisis pregnancies that I was confident in my vocational choice. Since graduating in 1994 with a Master's Degree in Social Work, I continue to explore how I will pursue my chosen vocation of helping others. I have found that working with students who are exploring their careers and life possibilities is extremely rewarding. I believe that finding one's purpose takes time and is an ever-evolving process. I can't wait to find out what I will be when I grow up.

References

Basalla, Susan and Debelius, Maggie. (2001). *So what are you going to do with that?: A guide to career-changing for M.A.'s and Ph.D's.* New York, NY: Farrar, Straus and Giroux.

Borgen, F. and Grutter, J. (1994). *Where do I go next?: Using your Strong results to manage your career.* Palo Alto, CA: Consulting Psychologists Press, Inc.

Bureau of Labor Statistics. (2002). *Occupational Outlook Handbook 2002-2003.* Retrieved July 30, 2002 from World Wide Web: http://www.bls.gov/oco/home.htm.

Bridges, William. (1995). *Jobshift: How to prosper in a workplace without jobs.* Cambridge, MA: Perseus Publishing.

Buckingham, Marcus and Clifton, Donald O. (2001). *Now, discover your strengths.* New York, NY: The Free Press.

Demarest, Larry. (1997). *Looking at Type in the workplace.* Palo Alto, CA: Consulting Psychologists Press, Inc.

Ditiberio, John K. and Hammer, Allen L. (1993). *Introduction to Type in College®.* Palo Alto, CA: Consulting Psychologists Press, Inc.

Dinklage, Lillian B. (1967). *Adolescent Choice and Decision-Making.* Cambridge, MA: Harvard University.

Dunning, Donna. (2001). *What's Your Type of Career?* Palo Alto, CA: Davies-Black Publishing.

Hammer, Allen L. (1993). *Introduction to Type and Careers®.* Palo Alto, CA: Consulting Psychologists Press, Inc.

Harris-Tuck, Price, A. and Robertson, M. (2000). *Career Patterns: A kaleidoscope of possibilities.* Upper Saddle River, NJ: Prentice Hall.

Johnston, Susan M. (1999). *The Career Adventure.* Upper Saddle River, NJ: Prentice Hall. (3rd ed.).

Jung, Carl G. (1971). *Psychological Types.* In Collected Works: Vol. 6 (R.F.C. Hull, Trans.). Princeton, NJ: Princeton University Press. (Originally published in German as Psychologische Typen, Rasher Verlag, Zurich, 1921) USA.

Laurence, D. Gordon, et al. (2001). *The MBTI® Qualifying Program Manual.* Gainesville, FL: Center for the Application of Psychological Type, Inc.

Martin, Charles. (1997). *Looking at Type: The fundamentals.* Gainesville, FL: Center for Application of Psychological Type, Inc.

Myers, Isabel B. (1998). *Introduction to Type®.* Palo Alto, CA: Consulting Psychologists Press, Inc.

Myers, Isabel B. and McCaulley, M. H. (1985). *Manual: A guide to the development and use of the Myers-Briggs Type Indicator®.* Palo Alto, CA: Consulting Psychologists Press, Inc.

Myers, Isabel B. et. al. (1998). *Manual: A guide to the development and use of the Myers-Briggs Type Indicator®.* Palo Alto, CA: Consulting Psychologists Press, Inc.

Montross, D.H., Leibowitz, Z.B., and Shinkman, C.J. (1995). *Real People, Real Jobs.* Palo Alto, CA: Davies-Black Publishing.

National Association of Colleges and Employers. (2001). *Job Outlook: The Perfect Candidate.* Retrieved July 25, 2002 from the World Wide Web: http://www.naceweb.org/pubs/JobOutlook/joboutlook2001/candidate.htm.

Prince, J.P. (1995). *Strong Interest Inventory Resource: Strategies for group and individual interpretations in college settings.* Palo Alto, CA: Consulting Psychologists Press, Inc.

Sharf, Richard S. (1992). *Applying Career Development Theory to Counseling.* Pacific Grove, CA: Brooks/Cole Publishing Company.

Super, D.E., Savickas, M.L. and Super C. (1996). A life-span, life-space approach to career development. In D. Brown, L. Brooks & Associates (Eds.), *Career choice and development* (3rd ed.). San Francisco, CA: Jossey-Bass Publishers.

Tieger, P.D. and Barron-Tieger, B. (2001). *Do What You Are.* Boston, MA: Little, Brown, and Company.

Wall Street Journal, Careers Section, Feb. 27, 1995.